Stéphane Mallarmé

THE POEMS IN VERSE

(Poésies)

Stéphane Mallarmé

THEPOEMSINVERSE

(Poésies)

Translation and notes by

Peter Manson

Library of Congress Cataloging-in-Publication Data

Mallarmé, Stéphane, 1842-1898.
  [Poems. English.]
  The poems in verse / Stephane Mallarme ; translation and notes by Peter
Manson.
      p. cm.
  Includes bibliographical references.
  ISBN 978-1-881163-50-3 (pbk.)
  I. Manson, Peter. II. Title.
  PQ2344.A2 2011
  841'.8--dc23
                              2011047753

Contents

The illustrations on pages 134 to 148 are by Jean-François Raffaelli, and are reproduced from the book *Les Types de Paris* (published by Plon, Nourrit et Cie for *Le Figaro*, Paris 1889). See the notes, p. 239, for more details.

Salut

Rien, cette écume, vierge vers
À ne désigner que la coupe;
Telle loin se noie une troupe
De sirènes mainte à l'envers.

Nous naviguons, ô mes divers
Amis, moi déjà sur la poupe
Vous l'avant fastueux qui coupe
Le flot de foudres et d'hivers;

Une ivresse belle m'engage
Sans craindre même son tangage
De porter debout ce salut

Solitude, récif, étoile
À n'importe ce qui valut
Le blanc souci de notre toile.

Greeting

No thing, this foam, a virgin verse
to outline nothing but the cup;
as, far away, a siren troupe
is drowned, and mainly bottoms-up.

My divers friends, we navigate,
me already on the poop-
deck, you the showboat prow that cuts
the winter flood-tide, thunder-struck;

a lovely drunkenness enlists
me, with no fear of pitch and toss
to bear upright this benison

solitude, reef, star
to whatever this is that was worth
the white disquiet of our cloth.

Le Guignon

Au-dessus du bétail ahuri des humains
Bondissaient en clartés les sauvages crinières
Des mendieurs d'azur le pied dans nos chemins.   3

Un noir vent sur leur marche éployé pour bannières
La flagellait de froid tel jusque dans la chair,
Qu'il y creusait aussi d'irritables ornières.   6

Toujours avec l'espoir de rencontrer la mer,
Ils voyageaient sans pain, sans bâtons et sans urnes,
Mordant au citron d'or de l'idéal amer.   9

La plupart râla dans les défilés nocturnes,
S'enivrant du bonheur de voir couler son sang,
Ô Mort le seul baiser aux bouches taciturnes!   12

Leur défaite, c'est par un ange très puissant
Debout à l'horizon dans le nu de son glaive:
Une pourpre se caille au sein reconnaissant.   15

Ils tètent la douleur comme ils tétaient le rêve
Et quand ils vont rythmant des pleurs voluptueux
Le peuple s'agenouille et leur mère se lève.   18

The Jinx

Above the dumbfounded human herd
the brilliant, savage manes of blue-
starved beggars leapt, their feet already in our way.

A black wind deployed as banner over their march
whipped it with cold so far into the flesh
that it hollowed irritable furrows.

Always in hope of arriving at the sea,
they voyaged without bread, or sticks, or urns,
biting the golden lemon of the bitter ideal.

Most grieved their last gasp in the night parades,
drunk on the joy of seeing their own blood flow,
O Death the only kiss for speechless mouths!

Their unmaking is in the hands of a potent angel,
his naked sword erect on the horizon:
a purple clot occludes the grateful breast.

They suck on pain as once they milked the dream:
when they give rhythmic form to carnal tears,
the people kneel down and their mother rises.

Ceux-là sont consolés, sûrs et majestueux;
Mais traînent à leurs pas cent frères qu'on bafoue,
Dérisoires martyrs de hasards tortueux.   21

Le sel pareil des pleurs ronge leur douce joue,
Ils mangent de la cendre avec le même amour,
Mais vulgaire ou bouffon le destin qui les roue.   24

Ils pouvaient exciter aussi comme un tambour
La servile pitié des races à voix ternes,
Égaux de Prométhée à qui manque un vautour!   27

Non, vils et fréquentant les déserts sans citerne,
Ils courent sous le fouet d'un monarque rageur,
Le Guignon, dont le rire inouï les prosterne.   30

Amants, il saute en croupe à trois, le partageur!
Puis le torrent franchi, vous plonge en une mare
Et laisse un bloc boueux du blanc couple nageur.   33

Grâce à lui, si l'un souffle à son buccin bizarre,
Des enfants nous tordront en un rire obstiné
Qui, le poing à leur cul, singeront sa fanfare.   36

Grâce à lui, si l'une orne à point un sein fané
Par une rose qui nubile le rallume,
De la bave luira sur son bouquet damné.   39

These ones are comforted, secure, majestic;
but a hundred jeered-at brothers dog their steps,
pathetic martyrs to contorted chance.

The same salt tears erode their gentle cheek,
they eat of ashes with the same devotion,
but the fate that guys them is vulgar or comic.

They too had power to excite, like drums,
the servile pity of a dull-voiced race,
peers of Prometheus without the vulture!

No, base and confined to deserts without cisterns,
they run beneath the scourge of a fractious monarch,
The Jinx, whose unheard-of laughter knocks them flat.

He leaps at lover's backs, to share the ride!
The torrent crossed, he dumps you in a pond,
leaving the two white swimmers blocked in mud.

Thanks to him, if someone blows a trumpet,
children will crack us up in wilful laughter
when, fist to arse, they ape its fanfare.

Thanks to him, if another, none too soon, should deck
a withered breast with a nubile rose, reviving it,
some spit will shine upon her damned bouquet.

Et ce squelette nain, coiffé d'un feutre à plume
Et botté, dont l'aisselle a pour poils vrais des vers,
Est pour eux l'infini de la vaste amertume. 42

Vexés ne vont-ils pas provoquer le pervers,
Leur rapière grinçant suit le rayon de lune
Qui neige en sa carcasse et qui passe au travers. 45

Désolés sans l'orgueil qui sacre l'infortune,
Et tristes de venger leurs os de coups de bec,
Ils convoitent la haine, au lieu de la rancune. 48

Ils sont l'amusement des racleurs de rebec,
Des marmots, des putains et de la vieille engeance
Des loqueteux dansant quand le broc est à sec. 51

Les poëtes bons pour l'aumône ou la vengeance,
Ne connaissant le mal de ces dieux effacés,
Les disent ennuyeux et sans intelligence. 54

« Ils peuvent fuir ayant de chaque exploit assez,
» Comme un vierge cheval écume de tempête
» Plutôt que de partir en galops cuirassés. 57

» Nous soûlerons d'encens le vainqueur dans la fête:
» Mais eux, pourquoi n'endosser pas, ces baladins,
» D'écarlate haillon hurlant que l'on s'arrête! » 60

And this dwarf skeleton, topped with a feathered hat,
in boots, whose armpit has real worms for hair,
is for them the infinity of vast bitterness.

Provoked, will they not prick at the pervert:
their creaking rapier follows the rays of moonlight
that snow into its corpse and pass on through.

Lacking the pride that glorifies bad fortune
and sad to avenge the pecking at their bones,
they covet hate, instead of nursing grudges.

They are the laughing stock of fiddle-scrapers,
of urchins, whores and of the eternal brood
of ragamuffins dancing when the bottle's dry.

The poets, always up for alms or vengeance,
not knowing these erased gods are sick,
say they are boring and without intelligence.

"They can run away, having had enough excitement,
as a virgin horse refuses foam and tempest
rather than galloping forth in armour.

We'll get the festal champion drunk on incense:
but they, why don't we make these minstrels take
to scarlet rags, howling for us to stop!"

Quand en face tous leur ont craché les dédains,
Nuls et la barbe à mots bas priant le tonnerre,
Ces héros excédés de malaises badins   63

Vont ridiculement se pendre au réverbère.

When everyone has spat scorn in their faces,
these heroes, overtired by playful sickness,
annulled men, praying for thunder in swallowed words

go hang themselves from the street lamp, laughably.

Apparition

La lune s'attristait. Des séraphins en pleurs
Rêvant, l'archet aux doigts dans le calme des fleurs
Vaporeuses, tiraient de mourantes violes
De blancs sanglots glissant sur l'azur des corolles
— C'était le jour béni de ton premier baiser.
Ma songerie aimant à me martyriser
S'enivrait savamment du parfum de tristesse
Que même sans regret et sans déboire laisse
La cueillaison d'un Rêve au cœur qui l'a cueilli.
J'errais donc, l'œil rivé sur le pavé vieilli
Quand avec du soleil aux cheveux, dans la rue
Et dans le soir, tu m'es en riant apparue
Et j'ai cru voir la fée au chapeau de clarté
Qui jadis sur mes beaux sommeils d'enfant gâté
Passait, laissant toujours de ses mains mal fermées
Neiger de blancs bouquets d'étoiles parfumées.

Apparition

The moon grew solemn. Seraphim in tears
dreaming, the bow held in their fingers, in the calm
of vaporous flowers, drew from fainting viols
white sobs to glide above the blue corollas
— it was the blessèd day of your first kiss.
My reverie, that loves to martyr me,
knowingly got drunk on the scent of sadness
that, even without regret or a bitter aftertaste, is left
by the harvest of a dream in the heart that harvested.
I wandered, then, my eyes fixed on the cobbles
when, with the sun in your hair, in the street,
in the evening, you appeared before me laughing
and my mind's eye saw the fairy with the cap of light
who passed over the nights of my spoiled childhood,
always allowing a snowstorm from her half-closed hands
of white bouquets of scented stars to fall.

Placet futile

Princesse! à jalouser le destin d'une Hébé
Qui poind sur cette tasse au baiser de vos lèvres,
J'use mes feux mais n'ai rang discret que d'abbé
Et ne figurerai même nu sur le Sèvres.

Comme je ne suis pas ton bichon embarbé,
Ni la pastille ni du rouge, ni Jeux mièvres
Et que sur moi je sais ton regard clos tombé,
Blonde dont les coiffeurs divins sont des orfèvres!

Nommez-nous.. toi de qui tant de ris framboisés
Se joignent en troupeau d'agneaux apprivoisés
Chez tous broutant les vœux et bêlant aux délires,

Nommez-nous.. pour qu'Amour ailé d'un éventail
M'y peigne flûte aux doigts endormant ce bercail,
Princesse, nommez-nous berger de vos sourires.

Futile Petition

Princess! jealous of the fate of a Hebe
dawning upon this cup when you kiss it,
I turn up the heat but have just the sober rank of curate
and won't even figure naked on the Sèvres.

Because I am not your bearded poodle,
pastille or rouge, or parlour-game,
and because I know your gaze fell closed on me,
blonde whose hairdresser is a silversmith!

Name us.. you, so much of whose raspberry laughter
joins in with a flock of tame lambs
grazing on everyone's vows, bleating at frenzies,

Name us.. so that Love winged with a fan
might paint me there, the flute held in my fingers, lulling the fold,
Princess, name us the shepherd of your smiles.

Le Pitre châtié

Yeux, lacs avec ma simple ivresse de renaître
Autre que l'histrion qui du geste évoquais
Comme plume la suie ignoble des quinquets,
J'ai troué dans le mur de toile une fenêtre.

De ma jambe et des bras limpide nageur traître,
À bonds multipliés, reniant le mauvais
Hamlet! c'est comme si dans l'onde j'innovais
Mille sépulcres pour y vierge disparaître.

Hilare or de cymbale à des poings irrité,
Tout à coup le soleil frappe la nudité
Qui pure s'exhala de ma fraîcheur de nacre,

Rance nuit de la peau quand sur moi vous passiez,
Ne sachant pas, ingrat! que c'était tout mon sacre,
Ce fard noyé dans l'eau perfide des glaciers.

The Clown Punished

Eyes, lakes with my simple yen to be reborn
other than as the ham whose gesture conjured up
as a plume the filthy oil-lamp's soot,
I have torn a window in the canvas wall.

A traitor, limpid swimmer, arm and leg
repeat their strokes, repudiating no-good
Hamlet! it is as if I invented in the wave
a thousand tombs to dive into, a virgin.

Hilarious gold of the cymbal beaten at by fists,
at once the sunlight strikes the nudity
that breathed out purely from my pearly freshness,

rancid night of the skin when you passed over me,
not knowing, ingrate! that my crowning glory
was greasepaint, drowned in deceit by glacial waters.

Une négresse par le démon secouée
Veut goûter une enfant triste de fruits nouveaux
Et criminels aussi sous leur robe trouée,
Cette goinfre s'apprête à de rusés travaux:

À son ventre compare heureuses deux tétines
Et, si haut que la main ne le saura saisir,
Elle darde le choc obscur de ses bottines
Ainsi que quelque langue inhabile au plaisir.

Contre la nudité peureuse de gazelle
Qui tremble, sur le dos tel un fol éléphant
Renversée elle attend et s'admire avec zèle,
En riant de ses dents naïves à l'enfant;

Et, dans ses jambes où la victime se couche,
Levant une peau noire ouverte sous le crin,
Avance le palais de cette étrange bouche
Pâle et rose comme un coquillage marin.

A negress shook up by the demon
would taste a child made sad by new fruits
and criminal with it under a threadbare shift;
the glutton's dressed for cunning stunts:

comparing two happy nipples on her belly,
so high no hand could intervene
she shoots the dark shock of her boots
like a tongue inept of pleasure.

Against the fearful gazelle-like nudity
that trembles, on her back, a mad elephant
upended to admire herself with zeal,
she waits, with naïve teeth laughing at the child;

and, between her legs where the victim's put to bed,
lifting a black skin open beneath the hair,
moves the palate of that strange mouth forward
pale and pink as a seashell.

Les Fenêtres

Las du triste hôpital, et de l'encens fétide
Qui monte en la blancheur banale des rideaux
Vers le grand crucifix ennuyé du mur vide,
Le moribond sournois y redresse un vieux dos,   4

Se traîne et va, moins pour chauffer sa pourriture
Que pour voir du soleil sur les pierres, coller
Les poils blancs et les os de la maigre figure
Aux fenêtres qu'un beau rayon clair veut hâler,   8

Et la bouche, fiévreuse et d'azur bleu vorace,
Telle, jeune, elle alla respirer son trésor,
Une peau virginale et de jadis! encrasse
D'un long baiser amer les tièdes carreaux d'or.   12

Ivre, il vit, oubliant l'horreur des saintes huiles,
Les tisanes, l'horloge et le lit infligé,
La toux; et quand le soir saigne parmi les tuiles,
Son œil, à l'horizon de lumière gorgé,   16

Voit des galères d'or, belles comme des cygnes,
Sur un fleuve de pourpre et de parfums dormir
En berçant l'éclair fauve et riche de leurs lignes
Dans un grand nonchaloir chargé de souvenir!   20

The Windows

Sick of the hospice, sick of fetid incense
rising from vapid whiteness in the curtains
towards the tall crucifix, bored of the empty wall,
the dying and sly man sets an old back upright

and drags it, less to warm his rottenness
than to see sunlight on the stones, to press
white hairs and the bones of his thin face
to the windows a beautiful bright ray would suntan

and the mouth, feverish, as avid of azure blue
as when, in youth, it went to breathe its treasure,
a virgin skin, long gone! befouls
the lukewarm golden panes with a long bitter kiss.

He lives a drunk, forgetting the horror of holy oils,
tisanes, the clock and the inflicted bed,
the cough; and when evening bleeds among the tiles,
his eye, on the horizon gorged with light,

sees golden galleys, beautiful as swans,
asleep on a fragrant, purple river,
rocking the wildcat lightning of their lines
in a grand indifference charged with memory!

Ainsi, pris du dégoût de l'homme à l'âme dure
Vautré dans le bonheur, où ses seuls appétits
Mangent, et qui s'entête à chercher cette ordure
Pour l'offrir à la femme allaitant ses petits,   24

Je fuis et je m'accroche à toutes les croisées
D'où l'on tourne l'épaule à la vie, et, béni,
Dans leur verre, lavé d'éternelles rosées,
Que dore le matin chaste de l'Infini   28

Je me mire et me vois ange! et je meurs, et j'aime
— Que la vitre soit l'art, soit la mysticité —
À renaître, portant mon rêve en diadème,
Au ciel antérieur où fleurit la Beauté!   32

Mais, hélas! Ici-bas est maître: sa hantise
Vient m'écœurer parfois jusqu'en cet abri sûr,
Et le vomissement impur de la Bêtise
Me force à me boucher le nez devant l'azur.   36

Est-il moyen, ô Moi qui connais l'amertume,
D'enfoncer le cristal par le monstre insulté
Et de m'enfuir, avec mes deux ailes sans plume
— Au risque de tomber pendant l'éternité?   40

So, seized by disgust for the man of obdurate soul
sprawled in happiness, where his appetites only
are fed, who persists in searching this filth
to offer it to the woman nursing his little ones,

I flee, and I cling to all cross-panes
where a man can show life the cold shoulder, and, blessed
in their glass, washed by eternal dews,
gilded by the chaste morning of the Infinite

in their mirror I see myself an angel! and I die, I love
— if the windowpane be art, or the mystical —
to be reborn, wearing my dream for a diadem,
in a prior sky where Beauty flourishes!

But alas! this world is master: its obsessive fear
comes even in this safe house to make me sick,
and the impure vomit of Stupidity
compels me to hold my nose before the blue.

Is there a means, o Self well-versed in bitterness,
to smash the crystal insulted by the monster
and to fly, with my two wings featherless
— at the risk of falling till the end of eternity?

Les Fleurs

Des avalanches d'or du vieil azur, au jour
Premier et de la neige éternelle des astres
Jadis tu détachas les grands calices pour
La terre jeune encore et vierge de désastres,   4

Le glaïeul fauve, avec les cygnes au col fin,
Et ce divin laurier des âmes exilées
Vermeil comme le pur orteil du séraphin
Que rougit la pudeur des aurores foulées,   8

L'hyacinthe, le myrte à l'adorable éclair
Et, pareille à la chair de la femme, la rose
Cruelle, Hérodiade en fleur du jardin clair,
Celle qu'un sang farouche et radieux arrose!   12

Et tu fis la blancheur sanglotante des lys
Qui roulant sur des mers de soupirs qu'elle effleure
À travers l'encens bleu des horizons pâlis
Monte rêveusement vers la lune qui pleure!   16

Hosannah sur le cistre et dans les encensoirs,
Notre dame, hosannah du jardin de nos limbes!
Et finisse l'écho par les célestes soirs,
Extase des regards, scintillement des nimbes!   20

The Flowers

On the first day, long ago, you broke
off from the golden landslides of old blue
and from the eternal snow of stars, great calices
for the still young earth, a virgin of disasters;

fauve gladiolus, with the thin-necked swans,
and this divine laurel of exiled souls
vermilion as the pure toe of the seraphim
flushed with the modesty of walked-on dawns,

the hyacinth, the lovely, glinting myrtle
and, equal to a woman's flesh, the cruel
rose, Hérodiade flower of the bright garden,
watered by a fierce and radiant blood!

You made the sobbing whiteness of the lily
that, brushing on the rolling sea of sighs,
through the blue incense of the pale horizons
dreamily rises towards the weeping moon!

Hosanna on the lute and in the censers,
Our lady, hosanna from the garden of our limbo!
Let the echo end through the celestial evenings,
ecstatic glances, scintillating haloes!

Ô Mère, qui créas en ton sein juste et fort,
Calices balançant la future fiole,
De grandes fleurs avec la balsamique Mort
Pour le poëte las que la vie étiole.   24

O Mother who created in your strong, just breast
calices balancing the future phial,
giant flowers with balsamic Death
for the tired poet whom life etiolates.

Renouveau

Le printemps maladif a chassé tristement
L'hiver, saison de l'art serein, l'hiver lucide,
Et dans mon être à qui le sang morne préside
L'impuissance s'étire en un long bâillement.

Des crépuscules blancs tiédissent sous mon crâne
Qu'un cercle de fer serre ainsi qu'un vieux tombeau,
Et, triste, j'erre après un rêve vague et beau,
Par les champs où la sève immense se pavane

Puis je tombe énervé de parfums d'arbres, las,
Et creusant de ma face une fosse à mon rêve,
Mordant la terre chaude où poussent les lilas,

J'attends, en m'abîmant que mon ennui s'élève…
— Cependant l'Azur rit sur la haie et l'éveil
De tant d'oiseaux en fleur gazouillant au soleil.

Renewal

Sadly, the sickly spring has seen off winter,
winter, season of calm art, lucid winter,
and in my being where drab blood presides,
impotence stretches itself in one big yawn.

White twilights are going cold beneath my skullcap
gripped as a tomb is by an iron ring
and I wander, after a dream both vague and pleasing,
through fields where the rising sap-scape struts its stuff

then I tumble, sick of the perfumed saplings, weary,
digging my dream a grave with my own face,
biting the hot terrain where lilacs push

I wait, engulfed, for signs of lifting boredom...
— but the sky laughs over the hedgerow and the awakening
of so many birds into flower, singing in sun.

Angoisse

Je ne viens pas ce soir vaincre ton corps, ô bête
En qui vont les péchés d'un peuple, ni creuser
Dans tes cheveux impurs une triste tempête
Sous l'incurable ennui que verse mon baiser:

Je demande à ton lit le lourd sommeil sans songes
Planant sous les rideaux inconnus du remords,
Et que tu peux goûter après tes noirs mensonges,
Toi qui sur le néant en sais plus que les morts:

Car le Vice, rongeant ma native noblesse,
M'a comme toi marqué de sa stérilité,
Mais tandis que ton sein de pierre est habité

Par un cœur que la dent d'aucun crime ne blesse,
Je fuis, pâle, défait, hanté par mon linceul,
Ayant peur de mourir lorsque je couche seul.

Anguish

I don't come tonight to lay your body, beast
hosting the sins of a people, nor to dig
a sullen tempest in your impure hair
using the boredom I transmit by kissing:

I ask of your bed a heavy, dreamless sleep
blank under curtains unconscious of remorse,
that you, all black lies told, can taste,
you who know more about nothingness than the dead:

for Vice, eating into my native nobility
has marked me out, like you, for its sterility
but, while your breast of stone is home

to a heart the tooth of no crime wounds,
I flee, unmade, pale, haunted by my shroud,
afraid of dying when I sleep alone.

Las de l'amer repos où ma paresse offense
Une gloire pour qui jadis j'ai fui l'enfance
Adorable des bois de roses sous l'azur
Naturel, et plus las sept fois du pacte dur
De creuser par veillée une fosse nouvelle   5
Dans le terrain avare et froid de ma cervelle,
Fossoyeur sans pitié pour la stérilité,
— Que dire à cette Aurore, ô Rêves, visité
Par les roses, quand, peur de ses roses livides,
Le vaste cimetière unira les trous vides? —   10
Je veux délaisser l'Art vorace d'un pays
Cruel, et, souriant aux reproches vieillis
Que me font mes amis, le passé, le génie,
Et ma lampe qui sait pourtant mon agonie,
Imiter le Chinois au cœur limpide et fin   15
De qui l'extase pure est de peindre la fin
Sur ses tasses de neige à la lune ravie
D'une bizarre fleur qui parfume sa vie
Transparente, la fleur qu'il a sentie, enfant,
Au filigrane bleu de l'âme se greffant.   20
Et, la mort telle avec le seul rêve du sage,
Serein, je vais choisir un jeune paysage
Que je peindrais encor sur les tasses, distrait.
Une ligne d'azur mince et pâle serait
Un lac, parmi le ciel de porcelaine nue,   25

Sick of unquiet rest, where my idleness offends
a fame I fled to once from the adorable
infancy of rose-woods under natural
blue, seven times more sick of the hard bargain
of hollowing one new grave per sleepless night
in my brain's cold avaricious territory,
gravedigger who has no pity for sterility,
— what to say to this Dawn, o Dreams, visited
by roses, when, in fear of its livid roses,
the vast necropolis will unite all holes? —
I want to have done with the voracious Art
of a cruel land, to shrug off the reproaches
of genius and the past, my outmoded allies,
and the lamp which at least knows all my agony,
to imitate that limpid Chinese heart
whose purest ecstasy is to paint
on cups of snow abducted from the moon
an end to the flower that perfumes his transparent
life, the same strange flower he sensed in childhood,
ingrafted to the soul's blue watermark.
With such a death, the sage's only dream,
serenely, I will choose a young landscape
to paint abstractedly upon the cups.
A pale, thin line of blue would be
a lake, set in the sky of naked china,

Un clair croissant perdu par une blanche nue
Trempe sa corne calme en la glace des eaux,
Non loin de trois grands cils d'émeraude, roseaux.

a crescent moon eclipsed by cloud
quenches its calm, white horn in the ice of waters,
not far from three long green eyelashes, reeds.

Le Sonneur

Cependant que la cloche éveille sa voix claire
À l'air pur et limpide et profond du matin
Et passe sur l'enfant qui jette pour lui plaire
Un angelus parmi la lavande et le thym,

Le sonneur effleuré par l'oiseau qu'il éclaire,
Chevauchant tristement en geignant du latin
Sur la pierre qui tend la corde séculaire,
N'entend descendre à lui qu'un tintement lointain.

Je suis cet homme. Hélas! de la nuit désireuse,
J'ai beau tirer le câble à sonner l'Idéal,
De froids péchés s'ébat un plumage féal,

Et la voix ne me vient que par bribes et creuse!
Mais, un jour, fatigué d'avoir enfin tiré,
Ô Satan, j'ôterai la pierre et me pendrai.

Bell Ringer

While the bell awakens its clear voice
to the pure and limpid, deep air of the morning,
passing over the child, who sings to please it
an angelus among lavender and thyme,

the ringer, brushed by the bird he brings to light,
sitting astride morosely — muttering Latin —
the stone that tightens the rope of centuries,
at his end only hears a distant tinkling.

I am this man. Alas! well might I pull
the cord of anxious night to sound the Ideal:
the faithful feathers of cold sins are stirring,

and the voice comes to me fitfully, and hollow!
But one day, tired from having pulled at last,
Satan, I'll be the stone and hang myself.

Tristesse d'été

Le soleil, sur le sable, ô lutteuse endormie,
En l'or de tes cheveux chauffe un bain langoureux
Et, consumant l'encens sur ta joue ennemie,
Il mêle avec les pleurs un breuvage amoureux.

De ce blanc flamboiement l'immuable accalmie
T'a fait dire, attristée, ô mes baisers peureux
« Nous ne serons jamais une seule momie
Sous l'antique désert et les palmiers heureux! »

Mais la chevelure est une rivière tiède,
Où noyer sans frissons l'âme qui nous obsède
Et trouver ce Néant que tu ne connais pas.

Je goûterai le fard pleuré par tes paupières,
Pour voir s'il sait donner au cœur que tu frappas
L'insensibilité de l'azur et des pierres.

Summer Sadness

The sun runs a lazy tub in your hair's goldness,
fighter, asleep on the sand,
and, burning incense on your traitor jowl,
folds-in your tears to a love-potion.

The changeless lull of this white blaze
— o timid kiss! — has made you say in sadness:
"never shall we rest, a lonely mummy
 under the antique desert and the happy palms!"

But your hair's a lukewarm river:
a place for drowning, coldly, the soul that haunts us
and for finding this Nothingness you do not know!

I'll lick the shadow from your lidded eyes
to see if it will lend the heart you battered
the insensibility of the stones and sky.

L'Azur

De l'éternel Azur la sereine ironie
Accable, belle indolemment comme les fleurs,
Le poëte impuissant qui maudit son génie
À travers un désert stérile de Douleurs.   4

Fuyant, les yeux fermés, je le sens qui regarde
Avec l'intensité d'un remords atterrant,
Mon âme vide. Où fuir? Et quelle nuit hagarde
Jeter, lambeaux, jeter sur ce mépris navrant?   8

Brouillards, montez! versez vos cendres monotones
Avec de longs haillons de brume dans les cieux
Que noiera le marais livide des automnes,
Et bâtissez un grand plafond silencieux!   12

Et toi, sors des étangs léthéens et ramasse
En t'en venant la vase et les pâles roseaux,
Cher Ennui, pour boucher d'une main jamais lasse
Les grands trous bleus que font méchamment les oiseaux.   16

Encor! que sans répit les tristes cheminées
Fument, et que de suie une errante prison
Éteigne dans l'horreur de ses noires traînées
Le soleil se mourant jaunâtre à l'horizon!   20

The Blue

The calm irony of the eternal Blue,
finely indolent as flowers, overwhelms
the impotent poet, cursing his genius
through a sterile desert of Pain.

Fleeing, with closed eyes, I can still sense it watching
my empty soul with the intensity of complete
remorse. But fly where? What wild night
can be thrown, what tatters, thrown on this nagging scorn?

Assemble, fogs! pour your self-coloured cinders
with long rags of mist into the sky
that the livid autumn marsh will drown
and build a great silencing ceiling!

And you, Dear Boredom, leave lethean ponds and gather
in passing the mud and the pallid reeds,
to plug with unwearying hand
the big blue holes the birds punched out on purpose.

Again! let sad chimneys smoke incessantly,
and let a wandering prison of soot
extinguish in the horror of its black trail
the sallow sun expiring on the horizon!

— Le Ciel est mort. — Vers toi, j'accours! Donne, ô matière,
L'oubli de l'Idéal cruel et du Péché
À ce martyr qui vient partager la litière
Où le bétail heureux des hommes est couché,   24

Car j'y veux, puisque enfin ma cervelle, vidée
Comme le pot de fard gisant au pied d'un mur,
N'a plus l'art d'attifer la sanglotante idée,
Lugubrement bâiller vers un trépas obscur..   28

En vain! l'Azur triomphe, et je l'entends qui chante
Dans les cloches. Mon âme, il se fait voix pour plus
Nous faire peur avec sa victoire méchante,
Et du métal vivant sort en bleus angelus!   32

Il roule par la brume, ancien et traverse
Ta native agonie ainsi qu'un glaive sûr;
Où fuir dans la révolte inutile et perverse?
Je suis hanté. L'Azur! l'Azur! l'Azur! l'Azur!   36

— The Sky is dead. — It is towards you I run! O matter,
delete all memory of the cruel Ideal and of Sin
in this martyr who comes to share the straw
where the happy herd of men is put to bed,

I want to be there, my brain, emptied at last
like a pot of greasepaint standing by the wall,
has no art left to retouch the tearful notion,
to yawn morosely towards an unknown death..

In vain! the Blue triumphs, and I hear it sing
in the bells. My soul, it makes itself a voice to make
us fear more after its spiteful victory
and exits the living metal in a blue angelus!

Ancient, it rolls with the fog, and penetrates
your native death-throes like a sharpened sword;
o where to fly in pointless and perverse revolt?
I am haunted. The Blue! The Blue! The Blue! The Blue!

Brise marine

La chair est triste, hélas! et j'ai lu tous les livres.
Fuir! là-bas fuir! Je sens que des oiseaux sont ivres
D'être parmi l'écume inconnue et les cieux!
Rien, ni les vieux jardins reflétés par les yeux
Ne retiendra ce cœur qui dans la mer se trempe
Ô nuits! ni la clarté déserte de ma lampe
Sur le vide papier que la blancheur défend,
Et ni la jeune femme allaitant son enfant.
Je partirai! Steamer balançant ta mâture
Lève l'ancre pour une exotique nature!
Un Ennui, désolé par les cruels espoirs,
Croit encore à l'adieu suprême des mouchoirs!
Et, peut-être, les mâts, invitant les orages
Sont-ils de ceux qu'un vent penche sur les naufrages
Perdus, sans mâts, sans mâts, ni fertiles îlots...
Mais, ô mon cœur, entends le chant des matelots!

Sea Breeze

The flesh is sad, and I've read all the books.
Away! away! I sense the birds are drunk
on being between the unknown foam and the skies!
Nothing, not the old gardens reflected in eyes
will hold back this sea-soaked heart,
o nights! not the desert brilliance of my lamp
on the empty paper defended by whiteness,
and not the young woman nursing her baby.
I will depart! Steamer, rocking your masts,
weigh anchor for an exotic nature!
A boredom, aggrieved by cruel hopes,
still believes in the last farewell of handkerchiefs!
And maybe the masts, inviting storms,
are the ones listing in wind above the shipwrecks
lost, with no masts, no masts, no fertile islets…
But hear, o heart, the master-singing sailors!

Soupir

Mon âme vers ton front où rêve, ô calme sœur,
Un automne jonché de taches de rousseur,
Et vers le ciel errant de ton œil angélique
Monte, comme dans un jardin mélancolique,
Fidèle, un blanc jet d'eau soupire vers l'Azur!
— Vers l'Azur attendri d'Octobre pâle et pur
Qui mire aux grands bassins sa langueur infinie:
Et laisse, sur l'eau morte où la fauve agonie
Des feuilles erre au vent et creuse un froid sillon,
Se traîner le soleil jaune d'un long rayon.

Sigh

My soul, calm sister, climbs towards your brow
where a freckled autumn dreams,
towards the vagrant sky of your angelic eye
as, faithful in a melancholic garden,
a jet of white water sighs towards the Blue!
— towards October's tender, pure, pale Blue
that mirrors infinite languor in great pools:
and allows, on dead water where lion-coloured leaves
vagrant in wind dig their own cold furrow,
the yellow sun to prolong itself in a ray.

Aumône

Prends ce sac, Mendiant! tu ne le cajolas
Sénile nourrisson d'une tétine avare
Afin de pièce à pièce en égoutter ton glas.   3

Tire du métal cher quelque péché bizarre
Et, vaste comme nous, les poings pleins, le baisons
Souffles-y qu'il se torde! une ardente fanfare.   6

Église avec l'encens que toutes ces maisons
Sur les murs quand berceur d'une bleue éclaircie
Le tabac sans parler roule les oraisons,   9

Et l'opium puissant brise la pharmacie!
Robes et peau, veux-tu lacérer le satin
Et boire en la salive heureuse l'inertie,   12

Par les cafés princiers attendre le matin?
Les plafonds enrichis de nymphes et de voiles,
On jette, au mendiant de la vitre, un festin.   15

Et quand tu sors, vieux dieu, grelottant sous tes toiles
D'emballage, l'aurore est un lac de vin d'or
Et tu jures avoir au gosier les étoiles!   18

Alms

Take this purse, beggar! you didn't cry for it,
senile nursling of a miser tit,
to milk your death-knell from it, bit by bit.

Beat the dear metal out into a sin
bizarre and vast, as we, our hands full, kiss it
and blow an ardent fanfare till it wriggles!

The houses are all made churches, walled with incense
when, cradling a blue break in the clouds,
silent tobacco rolls its orisons

and potent opium breaks the pharmacy!
Clothing and skin, do you want to rip the satin
and drink inertia in the happy spit,

waiting by princely cafés for the morning?
From ceilings rich with nymphs and veils
a feast is thrown to the beggar in the window.

And when, old god, you leave, shivering under canvas
wrapping, the dawn is a lake of golden wine
and you swear there are stars in your throat!

Faute de supputer l'éclat de ton trésor,
Tu peux du moins t'orner d'une plume, à complies
Servir un cierge au saint en qui tu crois encor.   21

Ne t'imagine pas que je dis des folies.
La terre s'ouvre vieille à qui crève la faim.
Je hais une autre aumône et veux que tu m'oublies   24

Et surtout ne va pas, frère, acheter du pain.

You can't compute the brilliance of your treasure,
but can smarten yourself with a feather, deliver
at compline a candle to the saint you believe in yet.

Don't imagine that I speak madness.
Earth opens old to one being killed by hunger.
I hate all other alms and want you to forget me:

above all, brother, don't go buying bread.

Don du poème

Je t'apporte l'enfant d'une nuit d'Idumée!
Noire, à l'aile saignante et pâle, déplumée,
Par le verre brûlé d'aromates et d'or,
Par les carreaux glacés, hélas! mornes encor,
L'aurore se jeta sur la lampe angélique.
Palmes! et quand elle a montré cette relique
À ce père essayant un sourire ennemi,
La solitude bleue et stérile a frémi.
Ô la berceuse, avec ta fille et l'innocence
De vos pieds froids, accueille une horrible naissance:
Et ta voix rappelant viole et clavecin,
Avec le doigt fané presseras-tu le sein
Par qui coule en blancheur sibylline la femme
Pour des lèvres que l'air du vierge azur affame?

Gift of the Poem

I bring to you the child of an Idumaean night!
Black with a bleeding and pale wing, plucked clean,
through the glass burnished by spice and gold,
through the frosted panes, alas! still in gloom,
dawn launched herself at the angelic lamp,
palms! and when she had shown this relic
to this father trying out a traitor smile,
blue and sterile solitude shuddered.
O cradle-rocker, with your daughter and the innocence
of your cold feet, welcome a horrible birth:
and your voice recalling viol and clavecin,
with a withered finger will you press the breast
through which flows in sibylline whiteness woman
for lips famished by virgin azure air?

Hérodiade

I: Ouverture ancienne d'Hérodiade

La Nourrice

(Incantation)

Abolie, et son aile affreuse dans les larmes
Du bassin, aboli, qui mire les alarmes,
De l'or nu fustigeant l'espace cramoisi,
Une Aurore a, plumage héraldique, choisi
Notre tour cinéraire et sacrificatrice,   5
Lourde tombe qu'a fuie un bel oiseau, caprice
Solitaire d'aurore au vain plumage noir...
Ah! des pays déchus et tristes le manoir!
Pas de clapotement! L'eau morne se résigne,
Que ne visite plus la plume ni le cygne   10
Inoubliable: l'eau reflète l'abandon
De l'automne éteignant en elle son brandon:
Du cygne quand parmi le pâle mausolée
Ou la plume plongea la tête, désolée
Par le diamant pur de quelque étoile, mais   15
Antérieure, qui ne scintilla jamais.

Crime! bûcher! aurore ancienne! supplice!
Pourpre d'un ciel! Étang de la pourpre complice!
Et sur les incarnats, grand ouvert, ce vitrail.

La chambre, singulière en un cadre, attirail   20

Hérodiade

I: Old overture of Hérodiade

The Nurse

(Incantation)

Abolished, and its frightful wing in the tears
of the pool, abolished, that mirrors the alarms,
flaying the crimson space of naked gold,
a Dawn, heraldic plumage, chose
our cinerary, sacrificing tower,
heavy tomb a beautiful bird has fled, lone
whim of dawn in vain black plumage...
Ah! sad and diminished country manor!
No plashing! The mournful water has given up,
no longer visited by feather or the unforgettable
swan: the water reflects the abandon
of autumn quenching his brand in it:
of the swan when into the pale mausoleum
or feathers the head plunged, aggrieved
by the pure diamond of some star, but
a prior one, that never scintillated.

Crime! immolation! ancient dawn! torture!
Purple of a sky! Pond complicit in purple!
and, wide open on the incarnadine, this stained glass.

The singular room in a frame, paraphernalia

De siècles belliqueux, orfèvrerie éteinte,
A le neigeux jadis pour ancienne teinte,
Et la tapisserie, au lustre nacré, plis
Inutiles avec les yeux ensevelis
De sibylles, offrant leur ongle vieil aux Mages.   25
Une d'elles, avec un passé de ramages
Sur ma robe blanchie en l'ivoire fermé
Au ciel d'oiseaux parmi l'argent noir parsemé,
Semble, de vols partis costumée et fantôme,
Un arôme qui porte, ô roses! un arôme,   30
Loin du lit vide qu'un cierge soufflé cachait,
Un arôme d'os froids rôdant sur le sachet,
Une touffe de fleurs parjures à la lune,
(À la cire expirée, encor s'effeuille l'une,)
De qui le long regret et les tiges de qui   35
Trempent en un seul verre à l'éclat alangui…
Une Aurore traînait ses ailes dans les larmes!

Ombre magicienne aux symboliques charmes!
Cette voix, du passé longue évocation,
Est-ce la mienne prête à l'incantation?   40
Encore dans les plis jaunes de la pensée
Traînant, antique, ainsi qu'une toile encensée
Sur un confus amas d'encensoirs refroidis,
Par les trous anciens et par les plis roidis
Percés selon le rythme et les dentelles pures   45
Du suaire laissant par ses belles guipures
Désespéré monter le vieil éclat voilé
S'élève, (ô quel lointain en ces appels celé!)

of warlike centuries, goldsmiths' faded work,
has the snow-bound past for its former colour,
and the tapestry, of nacreous lustre, useless
folds with the buried eyes
of sibyls offering their old fingernail to the Magi.
One of them, with embroidery of leaves
on my robe bleached in ivory, closed
to a sky of birds scattered on black silver,
seems, dressed in departed flights and ghostlike,
an aroma that carries, o roses! an aroma,
far from the empty bed a blown-out candle hid,
an aroma of cold bones creeping over the sachet,
a tuft of flowers sworn falsely to the moon,
(into expired wax one still drops its petals),
whose long regret and the stems of which
soak in a single glass in languid brilliance…
a Dawn was dragging its wings in the tears!

Magician shadow with symbolic charms!
This voice, long evocation of the past,
is it mine, ready for the incantation?
Still dragging in the yellow folds of thought,
antique, as a cloth of incense
on a confused mass of cooling church utensils,
through ancient holes and through the stiffened folds
pierced rhythmically and the pure lace
of the shroud, allowing through its fine crochet
the old veiled brilliance desperately to climb,
it is raised: (o, what a distance hidden in these calls!)

Le vieil éclat voilé du vermeil insolite,
De la voix languissant, nulle, sans acolyte, 50
Jettera-t-il son or par dernières splendeurs,
Elle, encore, l'antienne aux versets demandeurs,
À l'heure d'agonie et de luttes funèbres!
Et, force du silence et des noires ténèbres,
Tout rentre également en l'ancien passé, 55
Fatidique, vaincu, monotone, lassé,
Comme l'eau des bassins anciens se résigne.

Elle a chanté, parfois incohérente, signe
Lamentable!
    le lit aux pages de vélin,
Tel, inutile et si claustral, n'est pas le lin! 60
Qui des rêves par plis n'a plus le cher grimoire,
Ni le dais sépulcral à la déserte moire,
Le parfum des cheveux endormis. L'avait-il?
Froide enfant, de garder en son plaisir subtil
Au matin grelottant de fleurs, ses promenades, 65
Et quand le soir méchant a coupé les grenades!
Le croissant, oui le seul est au cadran de fer
De l'horloge, pour poids suspendant Lucifer,
Toujours blesse, toujours une nouvelle heurée,
Par la clepsydre à la goutte obscure pleurée, 70
Que, délaissée, elle erre, et, sur son ombre, pas
Un ange accompagnant son indicible pas!
Il ne sait pas cela, le roi qui salarie
Depuis longtemps la gorge ancienne et tarie.
Son père ne sait pas cela, ni le glacier 75

the old veiled brilliance of the unwonted gilding
of the voice, languishing, null, without acolyte,
will it throw down its gold among final splendours,
ever the antiphon to plaintiff hymns
in the hour of agony and death-struggles!
And, by the power of silence and black shadows,
all returns equally into the ancient past,
prophetic, vanquished, monotonous, tired
as the water of ancient pools gives up.

It has sung, sometimes incoherently, lamentable
sign!
     the bed with vellum pages,
useless and monastic, as linen is not!
No more does each fold bear the dear grammar-book of dreams,
nor the sepulchral canopy in desert silk
the perfume of sleeping hair. Did it have that?
Child cold from keeping for her subtle pleasure
her walks in the morning shivering with flowers,
and when spiteful evening has cut the pomegranates!
The crescent, yes the only one, on the iron face
of the clock, for a weight suspending Lucifer,
always wounds, always a new hour
wept in a dark drop by the clepsydra,
when she, abandoned, wanders, and in her shadow not
one angel to attend her unspeakable step!
The king does not know this, who for so long
has paid the ancient, dried-up breasts.
Her father does not know this, nor the fierce

Farouche reflétant de ses armes l'acier,
Quand, sur un tas gisant de cadavres sans coffre
Odorant de résine, énigmatique, il offre
Ses trompettes d'argent obscur aux vieux sapins!
Reviendra-t-il un jour des pays cisalpins!   80
Assez tôt? car tout est présage et mauvais rêve!
À l'ongle qui parmi le vitrage s'élève
Selon le souvenir des trompettes, le vieux
Ciel brûle, et change un doigt en un cierge envieux.
Et bientôt sa rougeur de triste crépuscule   85
Pénétrera du corps la cire qui recule!
De crépuscule, non, mais de rouge lever,
Lever du jour dernier qui vient tout achever,
Si triste se débat, que l'on ne sait plus l'heure
La rougeur de ce temps prophétique qui pleure   90
Sur l'enfant, exilée en son cœur précieux
Comme un cygne cachant en sa plume ses yeux,
Comme les mit le vieux cygne en sa plume, allée
De la plume détresse, en l'éternelle allée
De ses espoirs, pour voir les diamants élus   95
D'une étoile, mourante, et qui ne brille plus!

Et…

glacier reflecting his steel armoury,
when over a pile of corpses with no coffins
smelling of resin, enigmatic, he offers
his dark and silver trumpets to the old pine trees!
Will he come back one day from cisalpine lands!
Soon enough? for all is omen and bad dream!
On the fingernail lifted in the stained glass window
according to the memory of the trumpets, the old
sky burns, changing a finger to an envious candle.
And soon its redness as of mournful twilight
will penetrate the shrinking body of wax!
Of twilight, no, but of red dawn,
break of the last day come to end it all,
it struggles so sad one no longer knows the hour,
the red of this prophetic time, weeping
over the child, exiled in her precious heart
like a swan hiding its eyes in its feathers,
as the old swan placed them in its feathers, gone,
distress of the feathers, down the eternal avenue
of her hopes, to see the diamonds chosen
by a dying star, which no longer shines!

And...

II: Scène

La Nourrice — Hérodiade

N

Tu vis! ou vois-je ici l'ombre d'une princesse?
À mes lèvres tes doigts et leurs bagues, et cesse
De marcher dans un âge ignoré..

H

                 Reculez.
Le blond torrent de mes cheveux immaculés,
Quand il baigne mon corps solitaire le glace   5
D'horreur, et mes cheveux que la lumière enlace
Sont immortels. Ô femme, un baiser me tûrait
Si la beauté n'était la mort..

                     Par quel attrait
Menée et quel matin oublié des prophètes
Verse, sur les lointains mourants, ses tristes fêtes,   10
Le sais-je? tu m'as vue, ô nourrice d'hiver,
Sous la lourde prison de pierres et de fer
Où de mes vieux lions traînent les siècles fauves
Entrer, et je marchais, fatale, les mains sauves,
Dans le parfum désert de ces anciens rois: 15
Mais encore as-tu vu quels furent mes effrois?
Je m'arrête rêvant aux exils, et j'effeuille,
Comme près d'un bassin dont le jet d'eau m'accueille,

II: Scene

The Nurse — Hérodiade

N

You're alive! or is it the shade of a princess I see here?
To my lips with your fingers and their rings, and stop
walking in an unknown age..

H

Get back.
The blond torrent of my spotless hair
when it bathes my solitary body freezes it
with horror, and each hair, wound up in light
is immortal. O woman, a kiss would kill me
if beauty were not death..

By what lure
drawn and what morning forgotten by the prophets
pours its sad feasts on the dying distances —
do I know? you have seen me, winter nurse,
enter the heavy prison of stones and iron
where the wildcat centuries of my old lions drag
and I walked, fated, my hands unharmed,
in the desert perfume of those former kings:
but have you already seen what my fears were?
I halt, dreaming of exiles, and unpetal,
as if by a pool whose fountain welcomes me,

Les pâles lys qui sont en moi, tandis qu'épris
De suivre du regard les languides débris   20
Descendre, à travers ma rêverie en silence,
Les lions, de ma robe écartent l'indolence
Et regardent mes pieds qui calmeraient la mer.
Calme, toi, les frissons de ta sénile chair,
Viens et ma chevelure imitant les manières   25
Trop farouches qui font votre peur des crinières,
Aide-moi, puisqu'ainsi tu n'oses plus me voir,
À me peigner nonchalamment dans un miroir.

N

Sinon la myrrhe gaie en ses bouteilles closes,
De l'essence ravie aux vieillesses de roses   30
Voulez-vous, mon enfant, essayer la vertu
Funèbre?

H

    Laisse là ces parfums! Ne sais-tu
Que je les hais, nourrice, et veux-tu que je sente
Leur ivresse noyer ma tête languissante?
Je veux que mes cheveux qui ne sont pas des fleurs   35
À répandre l'oubli des humaines douleurs,
Mais de l'or, à jamais vierge des aromates,
Dans leurs éclairs cruels et dans leurs pâleurs mates,
Observent la froideur stérile du métal,
Vous ayant reflétés, joyaux du mur natal,   40

the pale lilies that are in me, while, following
with love-struck eyes the languid fragments
falling in silence through my reverie,
the lions, sweeping aside my lazy robe,
look at my feet that would becalm the sea.
Calm the shivering of your senile flesh:
come while my hair adopts the too savage
style that reminds you of your fear of manes,
and help me, since you dare not see me so,
to comb it nonchalantly in a mirror.

N

If not bright myrrh in its sealed bottles, my child,
would you like to try the funereal
virtues of essence stolen from the old age
of roses?

H

      Less of these perfumes! Do you not know
I hate them, nurse, and would you have me feel
their stupefaction drown my languishing head?
I want my hairs, which are not flowers
that spread forgetfulness of human sorrows,
but gold, forever virgin of aromatics,
in their cruel glint and their matt pallor,
to observe the sterile coldness of metal,
having reflected you, jewels of the natal wall,

Armes, vases, depuis ma solitaire enfance.

N

Pardon! l'âge effaçait, reine, votre défense
De mon esprit pâli comme un vieux livre ou noir..

H

Assez! Tiens devant moi ce miroir.
                                Ô miroir!
Eau froide par l'ennui dans ton cadre gelée   45
Que de fois et pendant les heures, désolée
Des songes et cherchant mes souvenirs qui sont
Comme des feuilles sous ta glace au trou profond,
Je m'apparus en toi comme une ombre lointaine.
Mais, horreur! des soirs, dans ta sévère fontaine,   50
J'ai de mon rêve épars connu la nudité!

Nourrice, suis-je belle?

N

Un astre, en vérité:
Mais cette tresse tombe..

H

Arrête dans ton crime

armour and vases since my solitary childhood.

N

Pardon! age had erased your prohibition, queen,
from my mind, faded like an old book or black..

H

Enough! Hold this mirror before me.
Mirror!
Cold water frozen in your frame by boredom,
how many times, and for hours, distressed
by dreams and searching my memories which are
like leaves in the deepest hole beneath your ice,
I appeared to myself in you as a distant shadow.
But, horror! some evenings, in your austere fountain,
I have known the nudity of my scattered dream!

Nurse, am I beautiful?

N

A star, truly:
but this tress is falling..

H

Arrest your crime

Qui refroidit mon sang vers sa source, et réprime
Ce geste, impiété fameuse: ah! conte-moi   55
Quel sûr démon te jette en ce sinistre émoi,
Ce baiser, ces parfums offerts et, le dirai-je?
Ô mon cœur, cette main encore sacrilège,
Car tu voulais, je crois, me toucher, font un jour
Qui ne finira pas sans malheur sur la tour..   60
Ô tour qu'Hérodiade avec effroi regarde!

N

Temps bizarre, en effet, de quoi le ciel vous garde!
Vous errez, ombre seule et nouvelle fureur,
Et regardant en vous précoce avec terreur;
Mais pourtant adorable autant qu'une immortelle,   65
Ô mon enfant, et belle affreusement, et telle
Que..

H

Mais n'allais-tu pas me toucher?

N

J'aimerais
Être à qui le Destin réserve vos secrets.

74

that chills my blood back to its source, and curb
that gesture, gross impiety: ah! tell me
what certain demon cast you in this sinister mood,
this kiss, these offered perfumes, and, will I say it?
O my heart, this once more sacrilegious hand,
for, I believe, you wanted to touch me, make a day
that will not end without misfortune over the tower..
O tower Hérodiade looks upon with dread!

N

Strange times, indeed, and heaven protect you from them!
You wander, a solo shadow and new fury,
looking inside your self, precocious with terror;
but ever adorable as an immortal,
my child, and fearfully beautiful and such
that..

H

But were you not going to touch me?

N

I would love
to serve the one for whom Fate keeps your secrets.

H

Oh! tais-toi!

N

Viendra-t-il parfois?

H

                              Étoiles pures,
N'entendez pas!

N

          Comment, sinon parmi d'obscures   70
Épouvantes, songer plus implacable encor
Et comme suppliant le dieu que le trésor
De votre grâce attend! Et pour qui, dévorée
D'angoisse, gardez-vous la splendeur ignorée
Et le mystère vain de votre être?   75

H

                    Pour moi.

N

Triste fleur qui croît seule et n'a pas d'autre émoi
Que son ombre dans l'eau vue avec atonie.

H

Oh! shut up!

N

Will he come one day?

H

Pure stars,
do not listen!

N

How, except among shadowy
terrors, to imagine still more implacable
and like a supplicant the god for whom
the treasure of your grace is waiting! And for whom, eaten up
by anguish, do you keep the unknown splendour
and empty mystery of your being?

H

For me.

N

Sad flower that grows alone and has no other emotion
than its shadow on the water seen listlessly.

H

Va, garde ta pitié comme ton ironie.

N

Toutefois expliquez: oh! non, naïve enfant,
Décroîtra, quelque jour, ce dédain triomphant..   80

H

Mais qui me toucherait, des lions respectée?
Du reste, je ne veux rien d'humain et, sculptée,
Si tu me vois les yeux perdus aux paradis,
C'est quand je me souviens de ton lait bu jadis.

N

Victime lamentable à son destin offerte!   85

H

Oui, c'est pour moi, pour moi, que je fleuris, déserte!
Vous le savez, jardins d'améthyste, enfouis
Sans fin dans de savants abîmes éblouis,
Ors ignorés, gardant votre antique lumière
Sous le sombre sommeil d'une terre première,   90
Vous, pierres où mes yeux comme de purs bijoux
Empruntent leur clarté mélodieuse, et vous,

H

Go, keep your pity with your irony.

N

Explain, though: oh! no, naïve child,
one day this triumphant disdain will fade..

H

But who would touch me? I am respected by lions.
Besides, I want nothing human, and, if you see me
sculpted, the eyes lost in paradise,
it is when I remember your milk I drank long ago.

N

Lamentable victim offered to her fate!

H

Yes, it's for me — for me — that I flower, deserted!
You know it, amethyst gardens, buried
endlessly in dazzled, learned gulfs,
unknown golds, hiding your antique light
under the sombre sleep of a primal earth,
you, stones from which my eyes' pure jewels
borrow melodious brilliance, and you

Métaux qui donnez à ma jeune chevelure
Une splendeur fatale et sa massive allure!
Quant à toi, femme née en des siècles malins   95
Pour la méchanceté des antres sibyllins,
Qui parles d'un mortel! selon qui, des calices
De mes robes, arôme aux farouches délices,
Sortirait le frisson blanc de ma nudité,
Prophétise que si le tiède azur d'été,   100
Vers lui nativement la femme se dévoile,
Me voit dans ma pudeur grelottante d'étoile,
Je meurs!

   J'aime l'horreur d'être vierge et je veux
Vivre parmi l'effroi que me font mes cheveux
Pour, le soir, retirée en ma couche, reptile   105
Inviolé, sentir en la chair inutile
Le froid scintillement de ta pâle clarté,
Toi qui te meurs, toi qui brûles de chasteté,
Nuit blanche de glaçons et de neige cruelle!

Et ta sœur solitaire, ô ma sœur éternelle,   110
Mon rêve montera vers toi: telle déjà,
Rare limpidité d'un cœur qui le songea,
Je me crois seule en ma monotone patrie,
Et tout, autour de moi, vit dans l'idolâtrie
D'un miroir qui reflète en son calme dormant   115
Hérodiade au clair regard de diamant..
Ô charme dernier, oui! je le sens, je suis seule.

metals that give to my young hair
a fatal splendour and its massive impetus!
As for you, woman born in malignant centuries
for the spite of sibylline caves,
who speak of a mortal! according to whom, from the calices
of my robes, aroma of fierce delights,
the white shiver of my nudity would exit,
prophecy that if the summer's lukewarm blue
towards which woman natively undresses,
sees me in my trembling starlike modesty,
I will die!

      I love the horror of being virgin and I want
to live inside the fear my hair causes me
so that, at evening, withdrawn on my couch, inviolate
reptile, I might feel in my useless flesh
the cold scintillation of your pale brilliance,
you on the point of death, you who burn with chastity,
white night of icicles and cruel snow!

And your solitary sister, o my eternal sister,
my dream will climb towards you: already so,
rare limpidity of a heart that dreamt it,
I think I am alone in my monotonous homeland
while all around me lives in the idolatry
of a mirror reflecting in its sleeping calm
Hérodiade of the clear diamond glance..
O final charm, yes! I feel it, I am alone.

Madame, allez-vous donc mourir?

                  Non, pauvre aïeule,
Sois calme, et, t'éloignant, pardonne à ce cœur dur,
Mais avant, si tu veux, clos les volets: l'azur   120
Séraphique sourit dans les vitres profondes,
Et je déteste, moi, le bel azur!
                      Des ondes
Se bercent et, là-bas, sais-tu pas un pays
Où le sinistre ciel ait les regards haïs
De Vénus qui, le soir, brûle dans le feuillage: 125
J'y partirais.
            Allume encore, enfantillage,
Dis-tu, ces flambeaux où la cire au feu léger
Pleure parmi l'or vain quelque pleur étranger
Et..

Maintenant?

       Adieu.
           Vous mentez, ô fleur nue
De mes lèvres!

N

Madame, are you going to die?

H

                    No, poor grandmother,
be calm, and as you leave, pardon this hard heart,
but first, if you will, close the shutters: the seraphic
blue smiles in the deep window-panes,
and I hate the beautiful blue!
                    Waves
rock and, far away, do you not know a country
where the sinister sky has the hated glances
of Venus, at evening, burning in the foliage:
I would go there.
                    Light again, childish
though you call me, those torches where wax
weeps strange tears from nimble fire among futile gold
and..

N

Now?

H

        Farewell.
                    O naked flower of my lips,
you are lying!

J'attends une chose inconnue
Ou, peut-être, ignorant le mystère et vos cris,
Jetez-vous les sanglots suprêmes et meurtris
D'une enfance sentant parmi les rêveries
Se séparer enfin ses froides pierreries.

I await an unknown thing
or, perhaps, not knowing the mystery and your cries,
you emit the supreme, bruised sobbing
of a childhood sensing among daydreams
its frigid gemstones separate at last.

III: Cantique de saint Jean

Le soleil que sa halte
Surnaturelle exalte
Aussitôt redescend
      Incandescent   4

Je sens comme aux vertèbres
S'éployer des ténèbres
Toutes dans un frisson
      À l'unisson   8

Et ma tête surgie
Solitaire vigie
Dans les vols triomphaux
      De cette faux   12

Comme rupture franche
Plutôt refoule ou tranche
Les anciens désaccords
      Avec le corps   16

Qu'elle de jeûnes ivres
S'opiniâtre à suivre
En quelque bond hagard
      Son pur regard   20

III: Canticle of Saint John

The sun whose halt
supernaturally exalts it
instantly redescends
   incandescent

I feel as if dark wings
spread in my vertebrae
all of a quiver
   in unison

and my head having leapt
lonely watchman
in the triumphal flights
   of this scythe

as frank rupture
rather holds in check or settles
the old argument
   with the body

than from drunken fasting
stubbornly maintains
its pure regard
   through a wild bounce

Là-haut où la froidure
Éternelle n'endure
Que vous le surpassiez
　　　　Tous ô glaciers　　　　　　　　　　24

Mais selon un baptême
Illuminée au même
Principe qui m'élut
　　　　Penche un salut.　　　　　　　　　28

up there where the eternal
ice cannot stand
all of you surpassing it
        glaciers

but in accordance with a baptism
illuminated by the same
principle that chose me
        tips its hat.

L'Après-midi d'vn favne

Églogve

Le Favne

Ces nymphes, je les veux perpétuer.

                       Si clair,
Leur incarnat léger, qu'il voltige dans l'air
Assoupi de sommeils touffus.

             Aimai-je un rêve?

Mon doute, amas de nuit ancienne, s'achève
En maint rameau subtil, qui, demeuré les vrais   5
Bois mêmes, prouve, hélas! que bien seul je m'offrais
Pour triomphe la faute idéale de roses —

Réfléchissons..

        ou si les femmes dont tu gloses
Figurent un souhait de tes sens fabuleux!
Faune, l'illusion s'échappe des yeux bleus   10
Et froids, comme une source en pleurs, de la plus chaste:
Mais, l'autre tout soupirs, dis-tu qu'elle contraste
Comme brise du jour chaude dans ta toison?

The Afternoon of a favn

Eclogve

The Favn

These nymphs, I want to have them perpetuated.

So bright
their light carnal tint, that it floats in the air
drowsy with tufted sleep.

Did I love a dream?

My doubt, a mass of old night, ends
in many a subtle branch which, by remaining the real woods,
proves, alas! that alone I offered myself
the ideal error of roses as a triumph —

Let us reflect..

or if the women you gloze
stand for a desire of your fabling senses!
Faun, the illusion escapes from the cold
blue eyes, like a spring in tears, of the one more chaste:
the other is all sighs, do you say, by contrast,
like the breeze of the hot day in your fleece?

Que non! par l'immobile et lasse pâmoison
Suffoquant de chaleurs le matin frais s'il lutte,   15
Ne murmure point d'eau que ne verse ma flûte
Au bosquet arrosé d'accords; et le seul vent
Hors des deux tuyaux prompt à s'exhaler avant
Qu'il disperse le son dans une pluie aride,
C'est, à l'horizon pas remué d'une ride,   20
Le visible et serein souffle artificiel
De l'inspiration, qui regagne le ciel.

Ô bords siciliens d'un calme marécage
Qu'à l'envi des soleils ma vanité saccage,
Tacites sous les fleurs d'étincelles, CONTEZ   25
« *Que je coupais ici les creux roseaux domptés*
» *Par le talent; quand, sur l'or glauque de lointaines*
» *Verdures dédiant leur vigne à des fontaines,*
» *Ondoie une blancheur animale au repos:*
» *Et qu'au prélude lent où naissent les pipeaux,*   30
» *Ce vol de cygnes, non! de naïades se sauve*
» *Ou plonge.. »*
            Inerte, tout brûle dans l'heure fauve
Sans marquer par quel art ensemble détala
Trop d'hymen souhaité de qui cherche le *la*:
Alors m'éveillerais-je à la ferveur première,   35
Droit et seul, sous un flot antique de lumière,
Lys! et l'un de vous tous pour l'ingénuité.

But no! through the immobile and weary swoon
suffocating the cool morning with heat if it struggles,
no water murmurs that is not poured by my flute
into the grove irrigated by harmonies; and the only wind
prompt to exhale from the two pipes before
it scatter sound in an arid shower,
is, on the horizon unmoved by a ripple,
the visible and calm, artificial breath
of inspiration, that regains the sky.

O Sicilian shores of a tranquil marsh
ransacked by my vanity equal to any sun's,
tacit under the sparking flowers, TELL
"how I was here cutting the hollow reeds, tamed
by talent; when, on the glaucous gold of distant
verdures consecrating their vine to the fountains,
an animal whiteness undulates at rest:
and how at the slow prelude where the pipes are born
this flight of swans, no! of naiads saves itself
or plunges.."
        Inert, all burns in the fallow hour
without marking by what art escaped together
too much hymen desired by him seeking the *la*:
Then will I awaken to the primal fervour,
erect and alone, under an antique flood of light,
lilies! and one of you, ingenuous.

Autre que ce doux rien par leur lèvre ébruité,
Le baiser, qui tout bas des perfides assure,
Mon sein, vierge de preuve, atteste une morsure   40
Mystérieuse, due à quelque auguste dent;
Mais, bast! arcane tel élut pour confident
Le jonc vaste et jumeau dont sous l'azur on joue:
Qui, détournant à soi le trouble de la joue,
Rêve, dans un solo long, que nous amusions   45
La beauté d'alentour par des confusions
Fausses entre elle-même et notre chant crédule;
Et de faire aussi haut que l'amour se module
Évanouir du songe ordinaire de dos
Ou de flanc pur suivis avec mes regards clos,   50
Une sonore, vaine et monotone ligne.

Tâche donc, instrument des fuites, ô maligne
Syrinx, de refleurir aux lacs où tu m'attends!
Moi, de ma rumeur fier, je vais parler longtemps
Des déesses; et, par d'idolâtres peintures,   55
À leur ombre enlever encore des ceintures:
Ainsi, quand des raisins j'ai sucé la clarté,
Pour bannir un regret par ma feinte écarté,
Rieur, j'élève au ciel d'été la grappe vide
Et, soufflant dans ses peaux lumineuses, avide   60
D'ivresse, jusqu'au soir je regarde au travers.

Ô nymphes, regonflons des SOUVENIRS divers.

Other than this sweet nothing their lip divulged,
the kiss, that softly assures of the perfidious ones,
my breast, virgin of proof, attests a mysterious
bitemark, owed to some noble tooth;
but enough! such an arcanum chose for confidant
the vast twin bulrush we play on under the blue:
that, turning the cheek's turmoil on itself
dreams, in a long solo, that we entertained
the surrounding beauty with some false
confusion between itself and our credulous song;
and of causing, as high as love attunes itself,
to evaporate from the usual dream of back
or pure flank followed by my closed glances,
a sonorous, empty and monotonic line.

Try then, instrument of flights, o malign
syrinx, to flower again on the lakes where you wait for me!
Proud of my murmuring, I will speak for ages
of goddesses, and by idolatrous paintings
remove again still more girdles from their shade:
just as, when I've sucked the brilliance out of grapes,
to banish a regret my ruse dismissed,
laughing, I lift the empty bunch to the summer sky,
and, breathing into its luminous skins, eager to be
drunk, I gaze through it till evening.

O nymphs, let us re-tumesce some divers MEMORIES.

« *Mon œil, trouant les joncs, dardait chaque encolure*
» *Immortelle, qui noie en l'onde sa brûlure*
» *Avec un cri de rage au ciel de la forêt;*   65
» *Et le splendide bain de cheveux disparaît*
» *Dans les clartés et les frissons, ô pierreries!*
» *J'accours; quand, à mes pieds, s'entrejoignent (meurtries*
» *De la langueur goûtée à ce mal d'être deux)*
» *Des dormeuses parmi leurs seuls bras hasardeux;*   70
» *Je les ravis, sans les désenlacer, et vole*
» *À ce massif, haï par l'ombrage frivole,*
» *De roses tarissant tout parfum au soleil,*
» *Où notre ébat au jour consumé soit pareil. »*
Je t'adore, courroux des vierges, ô délice   75
Farouche du sacré fardeau nu qui se glisse
Pour fuir ma lèvre en feu buvant, comme un éclair
Tressaille! la frayeur secrète de la chair:
Des pieds de l'inhumaine au cœur de la timide
Que délaisse à la fois une innocence, humide   80
De larmes folles ou de moins tristes vapeurs.
« *Mon crime, c'est d'avoir, gai de vaincre ces peurs*
» *Traîtresses, divisé la touffe échevelée*
» *De baisers que les dieux gardaient si bien mêlée;*
» *Car, à peine j'allais cacher un rire ardent*   85
» *Sous les replis heureux d'une seule (gardant*
» *Par un doigt simple, afin que sa candeur de plume*
» *Se teignît à l'émoi de sa sœur qui s'allume,*
» *La petite, naïve et ne rougissant pas:)*
» *Que de mes bras, défaits par de vagues trépas,*   90
» *Cette proie, à jamais ingrate, se délivre*

"My eye, piercing the reeds, fired at each immortal
neck, which drowns its burning in the wave
with a cry of rage to the forest sky;
and the splendid bath of hairs disappears
in the brilliancies and the shivering, o gemstones!
I run up; when at my feet are intertwined (bruised
by the languor tasted in this illness of being two)
women asleep among haphazard arms;
I seize, without untangling, them and fly
to this thicket, hated by frivolous shadow,
of roses drying their perfume in the sun
where our frolic might be, like the day, consumed."
I adore you, wrath of virgins, o fierce
delight of the sacred, naked burden that slips
to flee my lip on fire, drinking, as lightning
quivers! the secret fright of the flesh:
from the feet of the inhumane one to the heart of the timid
abandoned at once by an innocence, dampened
by mad tears or by less sad vapours.
"My crime is, happy at vanquishing these traitor
fears, to have parted the tousled tuft
of kisses the gods kept so well matted:
for, barely had I gone to hide an ardent laugh
under the happy folds of a single woman (detaining
with a simple finger, that her featherlike candour
be dipped in the emotion lighting up her sister,
the little one, naïve and unblushing:)
than from my arms, undone by vague deaths,
this prey, forever ingrate, frees itself

» Sans pitié du sanglot dont j'étais encore ivre. »

Tant pis! vers le bonheur d'autres m'entraîneront
Par leur tresse nouée aux cornes de mon front:
Tu sais, ma passion, que, pourpre et déjà mûre,   95
Chaque grenade éclate et d'abeilles murmure;
Et notre sang, épris de qui le va saisir,
Coule pour tout l'essaim éternel du désir.
À l'heure où ce bois d'or et de cendres se teinte
Une fête s'exalte en la feuillée éteinte: 100
Etna! c'est parmi toi visité de Vénus
Sur ta lave posant ses talons ingénus,
Quand tonne un somme triste ou s'épuise la flamme.
Je tiens la reine!

       Ô sûr châtiment...

                   Non, mais l'âme
De paroles vacante et ce corps alourdi   105
Tard succombent au fier silence de midi:
Sans plus il faut dormir en l'oubli du blasphème,
Sur le sable altéré gisant et comme j'aime
Ouvrir ma bouche à l'astre efficace des vins!

Couple, adieu; je vais voir l'ombre que tu devins.   110

without pity for the sobbing from which I was still drunk."

No matter! others will drag me to happiness
by their tresses knotted in the horns on my brow:
my passion, you know, that, purple and already ripe,
each pomegranate bursts and hums with bees;
and our blood, in love with what will seize it,
flows for all the eternal swarm of desire.
At the hour when this wood is dipped in gold and ashes
a feast takes fire in the extinct foliage:
Etna! it is upon you, visited by Venus
planting her artless heels on your lava,
when a sad sleep thunders or the flame gives out,
I hold the queen!

O certain punishment...

No, but the soul
emptied of words and this body grown heavy
succumb late to the proud silence of noon:
enough, let us sleep, forgetful of the blasphemy,
lying on the thirsty sand and as I love,
open my mouth to the effective star of wine!

Couple, farewell; I will see the shadow you became.

La chevelure vol d'une flamme à l'extrême
Occident de désirs pour la tout éployer
Se pose (je dirais mourir un diadème)
Vers le front couronné son ancien foyer

Mais sans or soupirer que cette vive nue
L'ignition du feu toujours intérieur
Originellement la seule continue
Dans le joyau de l'œil véridique ou rieur

Une nudité de héros tendre diffame
Celle qui ne mouvant astre ni feux au doigt
Rien qu'à simplifier avec gloire la femme
Accomplit par son chef fulgurante l'exploit

De semer de rubis le doute qu'elle écorche
Ainsi qu'une joyeuse et tutélaire torche

The hair a flame stealing away from the far
West of desires to unfold it all
alights (I would say a dying diadem)
towards the crowned brow its former hearth

but with no gold to sigh that this live cloud
the ignition of the fire always interior
originally the only one might continue
in the jewel of the eye veridic or laughing

to drape a hero's nudity defames
the one that moving neither star nor fire on finger
only by simplifying with glory the woman
achieves by lightning of her head the stroke

of sowing with rubies the doubt she flays
just like a joyous and tutelary torch

Sainte

À la fenêtre recélant
Le santal vieux qui se dédore
De sa viole étincelant
Jadis avec flûte ou mandore,

Est la Sainte pâle, étalant
Le livre vieux qui se déplie
Du Magnificat ruisselant
Jadis selon vêpre et complie:

À ce vitrage d'ostensoir
Que frôle une harpe par l'Ange
Formée avec son vol du soir
Pour la délicate phalange

Du doigt, que, sans le vieux santal
Ni le vieux livre, elle balance
Sur le plumage instrumental,
Musicienne du silence.

Saint

Concealing at the window-pane
the old, ungilding sandalwood
of her viol that once
sparkled with flute or mandola

is the pale Saint displaying
the old, unfolding book
of the Magnificat that once
streamed into vesper and compline:

at this monstrance window
brushed by a harp the Angel
made from its evening flight
for the delicate phalanx

of the finger, that, without sandalwood
or the old book, she posits
on the instrumental plumage,
musician of the silence.

Toast funèbre

Ô de notre bonheur, toi, le fatal emblème!

Salut de la démence et libation blême,
Ne crois pas qu'au magique espoir du corridor
J'offre ma coupe vide où souffre un monstre d'or!
Ton apparition ne va pas me suffire: 5
Car je t'ai mis, moi-même, en un lieu de porphyre.
Le rite est pour les mains d'éteindre le flambeau
Contre le fer épais des portes du tombeau:
Et l'on ignore mal, élu pour notre fête
Très-simple de chanter l'absence du poëte,   10
Que ce beau monument l'enferme tout entier:
Si ce n'est que la gloire ardente du métier,
Jusqu'à l'heure commune et vile de la cendre,
Par le carreau qu'allume un soir fier d'y descendre,
Retourne vers les feux du pur soleil mortel!   15

Magnifique, total et solitaire, tel
Tremble de s'exhaler le faux orgueil des hommes.
Cette foule hagarde! elle annonce: Nous sommes
La triste opacité de nos spectres futurs.
Mais le blason des deuils épars sur de vains murs,   20
J'ai méprisé l'horreur lucide d'une larme,
Quand, sourd même à mon vers sacré qui ne l'alarme,
Quelqu'un de ces passants, fier, aveugle et muet,

Funeral Toast

O fatal emblem, you, of our happiness!

Demented tribute, watered-down libation:
don't think that to the magic hope of the corridor
I offer my empty cup where a golden monster suffers!
Your apparition won't suffice for me
for I myself have put you in a place of porphyry.
The rite is for a hand to snuff the torch
against the thick iron portals of the tomb:
we know fine well, elected celebrants
who sing the simple absence of the poet,
that this fine monument encloses all of him:
were it not that the ardent glory of the calling
until the shared, ignoble hour of ashes,
through a window lit by an evening proud to fall there,
returns towards the fires of the pure mortal sun!

Magnificent, total and solitary, and such
as the bogus pride of men trembles to breathe.
The crowds are wild! now they announce: We are
the sad opacity of our future spectres.
Emblem of mourning scattered on empty walls,
I scorned the lucid horror of a tear,
when, deaf even to my sacred verse, and unalarmed,
one of these passers-by, proud, blind and mute,

Hôte de son linceul vague, se transmuait
En le vierge héros de l'attente posthume.   25
Vaste gouffre apporté dans l'amas de la brume
Par l'irascible vent des mots qu'il n'a pas dits,
Le néant à cet Homme aboli de jadis:
« Souvenir d'horizons, qu'est-ce, ô toi, que la Terre? »
Hurle ce songe; et, voix dont la clarté s'altère,   30
L'espace a pour jouet le cri: « Je ne sais pas! »

Le Maître, par un œil profond, a, sur ses pas,
Apaisé de l'éden l'inquiète merveille
Dont le frisson final, dans sa voix seule, éveille
Pour la Rose et le Lys le mystère d'un nom.   35
Est-il de ce destin rien qui demeure, non?
Ô vous tous! oubliez une croyance sombre.
Le splendide génie éternel n'a pas d'ombre.
Moi, de votre désir soucieux, je veux voir,
À qui s'évanouit, hier, dans le devoir,   40
Idéal que nous font les jardins de cet astre,
Survivre pour l'honneur du tranquille désastre
Une agitation solennelle par l'air
De paroles, pourpre ivre et grand calice clair,
Que, pluie et diamant, le regard diaphane   45
Resté là sur ces fleurs dont nulle ne se fane,
Isole parmi l'heure et le rayon du jour!

C'est de nos vrais bosquets déjà tout le séjour,
Où le poëte pur a pour geste humble et large
De l'interdire au rêve, ennemi de sa charge: 50

a guest in his baggy shroud, was self-transmuted
into the virgin hero of posthumous waiting.
Vast gulf delivered in a mass of fog
by the fractious wind of words he did not utter,
nothingness to this Man, long since abolished:
"Memory of horizons, you, O what is the Earth?"
the dream howls; in a voice of failing clearness,
toyed with by space, comes the cry: "I do not know!"

The Master, by a piercing eye, has, on his travels,
appeased the unquiet marvel that is Eden:
its final shiver, in his voice alone, awakens
for the Rose and Lily the mystery of a name.
Does nothing of this destiny remain, no?
O all of you, forget a dark belief:
the splendid, eternal genius has no shade.
I, who respect your will, I would see survive
of him who vanished in the ideal duty
made for us by the gardens of this star,
in honour of the undisturbed disaster,
a solemn agitation in the air
of words, drunken purple and great shining calyx
that, rain and diamond, the transparent glance
fallen upon these never-fading flowers
isolates in an hour and in the daylight ray!

It is the whole domain of our true grove
that the pure poet's humble, generous gesture
forbids to dreams, his function's enemy:

Afin que le matin de son repos altier,
Quand la mort ancienne est comme pour Gautier
De n'ouvrir pas les yeux sacrés et de se taire,
Surgisse, de l'allée ornement tributaire,
Le sépulcre solide où gît tout ce qui nuit,   55
Et l'avare silence et la massive nuit.

so that, the morning of his high repose,
when ancient death is, as for Gautier,
to not open sacred eyes and to stay silent,
in an aisle might rise the tributary adornment:
the solid sepulchre where all harm lies,
the miser silence and the massive night.

Prose

(pour des Esseintes)

Hyperbole! de ma mémoire
Triomphalement ne sais-tu
Te lever, aujourd'hui grimoire
Dans un livre de fer vêtu: 4

Car j'installe, par la science,
L'hymne des cœurs spirituels
En l'œuvre de ma patience,
Atlas, herbiers et rituels.   8

Nous promenions notre visage
(Nous fûmes deux, je le maintiens)
Sur maints charmes de paysage,
Ô sœur, y comparant les tiens.   12

L'ère d'autorité se trouble
Lorsque, sans nul motif, on dit
De ce midi que notre double
Inconscience approfondit   16

Que, sol des cent iris, son site,
Ils savent s'il a bien été,
Ne porte pas de nom que cite
L'or de la trompette d'Été.   20

Prose

(for des Esseintes)

Hyperbole! from my memory
triumphantly don't you know
how to raise yourself, today grammar
clad in a book in iron:

for I install, by science,
the heartfelt spiritual
in the labour of my patience,
atlas, herbal and ritual.

We took our face for a walk
(I maintain we were plural)
on the landscape's many charms,
O sister, to compare yours there.

The era of authority is flustered
when it is said, with no motive,
of this midday land our double
unwittingness came to dig

that, soil of a hundred irises, its site
— they know if it really existed —
bears no name cited by
the gold of Summer's trumpet.

Oui, dans une île que l'air charge
De vue et non de visions
Toute fleur s'étalait plus large
Sans que nous en devisions.   24

Telles, immenses, que chacune
Ordinairement se para
D'un lucide contour, lacune
Qui des jardins la sépara.   28

Gloire du long désir, Idées
Tout en moi s'exaltait de voir
La famille des iridées
Surgir à ce nouveau devoir,   32

Mais cette sœur sensée et tendre
Ne porta son regard plus loin
Que sourire et, comme à l'entendre
J'occupe mon antique soin.   36

Oh! sache l'Esprit de litige,
À cette heure où nous nous taisons,
Que de lis multiples la tige
Grandissait trop pour nos raisons   40

Et non comme pleure la rive,
Quand son jeu monotone ment
À vouloir que l'ampleur arrive
Parmi mon jeune étonnement   44

Yes, in an island charged by the air
with sight but not for seers
every flower loomed extra large
without our mentioning it:

All so immense that each one
ordinarily paraded
in a lucid contour, lacuna se-
parating it from the gardens.

Glory of the long desire, Ideas
all of them in me leapt to see
the family of the irides
arise to this new duty,

but that sane and tender sister
bent her regard no more sharply
than to smile, and as if attentive
I retake my former care.

Oh! Spirit of litigation, know,
in this our silent hour,
that the stem of multiplied lilies
outgrew our reasoning power

and not, as the water margin weeps,
when it rigs its monotonous game
that variety might arrive
in the midst of my young astonishment

D'ouïr tout le ciel et la carte
Sans fin attestés sur mes pas,
Par le flot même qui s'écarte,
Que ce pays n'exista pas.   48

L'enfant abdique son extase
Et docte déjà par chemins
Elle dit le mot: Anastase!
Né pour d'éternels parchemins,   52

Avant qu'un sépulcre ne rie
Sous aucun climat, son aïeul,
De porter ce nom: Pulchérie!
Caché par le trop grand glaïeul.   56

at hearing the whole sky and the map
without end made to swear on my footsteps,
even through the parting wave,
that this country did not exist.

The infant abdicates its ecstasy
and, dux of the ways already,
she says the word: Anastase!
born for eternal parchments,

before a sepulchre can laugh
in any latitude, its ancestor,
to bear this name: Pulcheria!
hidden by the too-large gladiolus.

Éventail

de Madame Mallarmé

Avec comme pour langage
Rien qu'un battement aux cieux
Le futur vers se dégage
Du logis très précieux

Aile tout bas la courrière
Cet éventail si c'est lui
Le même par qui derrière
Toi quelque miroir a lui

Limpide (où va redescendre
Pourchassée en chaque grain
Un peu d'invisible cendre
Seule à me rendre chagrin)

Toujours tel il apparaisse
Entre tes mains sans paresse

Fan

of Madame Mallarmé

With for language nothing
but a beat in the sky
the future verse breaks free
of the most precious dwelling

quiet wing the courier
this fan if it is the
same through which behind
you some mirror gleamed

limpidly (where invisible
ash pursued to the last grain
will fall back again
only to cause me pain)

may it always appear so
between your unlazy hands

Autre éventail

de Mademoiselle Mallarmé

Ô rêveuse, pour que je plonge
Au pur délice sans chemin,
Sache, par un subtil mensonge,
Garder mon aile dans ta main.   4

Une fraîcheur de crépuscule
Te vient à chaque battement
Dont le coup prisonnier recule
L'horizon délicatement.   8

Vertige! voici que frissonne
L'espace comme un grand baiser
Qui, fou de naître pour personne,
Ne peut jaillir ni s'apaiser.   12

Sens-tu le paradis farouche
Ainsi qu'un rire enseveli
Se couler du coin de ta bouche
Au fond de l'unanime pli!   16

Le sceptre des rivages roses
Stagnants sur les soirs d'or, ce l'est,
Ce blanc vol fermé que tu poses
Contre le feu d'un bracelet.   20

Another Fan

of Mademoiselle Mallarmé

Dreamer, that I might plunge
into pure unguided delight,
learn, by a subtle lie,
how to guard my wing in your hand.

A twilight coolness
comes your way with each beat
whose captive stroke delicately
pushes back the horizon.

Vertigo! see space
shivering like a great kiss
that, mad to have been born for no-one,
can neither break free nor calm down.

Do you feel the untamed paradise
slip like a buried laugh
from the corner of your mouth
to the base of the unanimous fold!

The sceptre of rose-coloured shores
stagnant on golden evenings, this is it,
this white closed flight you pose against
the fire of a bracelet.

Éventail

de Méry Laurent

De frigides roses pour vivre
Toutes la même interrompront
Avec un blanc calice prompt
Votre souffle devenu givre

Mais que mon battement délivre
La touffe par un choc profond
Cette frigidité se fond
En du rire de fleurir ivre

À jeter le ciel en détail
Voilà comme bon éventail
Tu conviens mieux qu'une fiole

Nul n'enfermant à l'émeri
Sans qu'il y perde ou le viole
L'arôme émané de Méry.

Fan

of Méry Laurent

Frigid roses to live
all for one will interrupt
your breath become frost
with a prompt white calyx

but if my strokes set the tuft
free by a profound shock
this frigidity will merge with
the laughter of drunken flowering

see, like a good fan
you are better than a phial
at casting the sky in fragments

no one can close in glass
without losing it or profaning
the aroma arisen from Méry.

Feuillet d'album

Tout à coup et comme par jeu
Mademoiselle qui voulûtes
Ouïr se révéler un peu
Le bois de mes diverses flûtes

Il me semble que cet essai
Tenté devant un paysage
A du bon quand je le cessai
Pour vous regarder au visage

Oui ce vain souffle que j'exclus
Jusqu'à la dernière limite
Selon mes quelques doigts perclus
Manque de moyens s'il imite

Votre très naturel et clair
Rire d'enfant qui charme l'air

Album Leaf

All at once as if in play
Mademoiselle who wanted to
hear the small revelation
of wood in my divers flutes

it seems to me this tentative
rehearsal before a landscape
turned out all right when I ended it
to look you in the face

yes this vain breath I exclude
to the ultimate stop
with my stiff little fingers
lacks the means to imitate

your so natural and clear
child's laugh charming the air

Remémoration d'amis belges

À des heures et sans que tel souffle l'émeuve
Toute la vétusté presque couleur encens
Comme furtive d'elle et visible je sens
Que se dévêt pli selon pli la pierre veuve

Flotte ou semble par soi n'apporter une preuve
Sinon d'épandre pour baume antique le temps
Nous immémoriaux quelques-uns si contents
Sur la soudaineté de notre amitié neuve

Ô très chers rencontrés en le jamais banal
Bruges multipliant l'aube au défunt canal
Avec la promenade éparse de maint cygne

Quand solennellement cette cité m'apprit
Lesquels entre ses fils un autre vol désigne
À prompte irradier ainsi qu'aile l'esprit.

Remembrance of Belgian Friends

At certain times without a breath of wind
all the dilapidation almost the colour of incense
as furtively and visibly of it I sense
the widowed stone divested fold by fold

floats or seems in itself to bring no proof
except to pour time for antique balm
on the suddenness of our new friendship
we immemorial someones so content

o dear ones met in never banal
Bruges multiplying dawn on the disused canal
by the scattered promenade of many swans

when solemnly this city showed me
those of its sons marked by another flight
to irradiate swiftly just like a wing the spirit.

Dame
            sans trop d'ardeur à la fois enflammant
La rose qui cruelle ou déchirée, et lasse
Même du blanc habit de pourpre, le délace
Pour ouïr dans sa chair pleurer le diamant

Oui, sans ces crises de rosée et gentiment
Ni brise quoique, avec, le ciel orageux passe
Jalouse d'apporter je ne sais quel espace
Au simple jour le jour très vrai du sentiment

Ne te semble-t-il pas, disons, que chaque année
Dont sur ton front renaît la grâce spontanée
Suffise selon quelque apparence et pour moi

Comme un éventail frais dans la chambre s'étonne
À raviver du peu qu'il faut ici d'émoi
Toute notre native amitié monotone.

Lady
> without too much ardour at once inflaming

the rose which cruel or in tatters, tired
even of the white habit unlaces it from purple
to hear the diamond weeping in its flesh

yes without these kindly crises of dew
or breeze though they make the stormy skies pass over
eager to bring I do not know what space
to the simple day the quite true day of sentiment

does it not seem to you, let us say, that each year
of grace reborn spontaneously on your brow
is enough whatever it looks like and for me

as a cool fan in the chamber is stunned
to revive with the little need for emotion here
all our native monotonous friendship.

Ô si chère de loin et proche et blanche, si
Délicieusement toi, Méry, que je songe
À quelque baume rare émané par mensonge
Sur aucun bouquetier de cristal obscurci

Le sais-tu, oui! pour moi voici des ans, voici
Toujours que ton sourire éblouissant prolonge
La même rose avec son bel été qui plonge
Dans autrefois et puis dans le futur aussi.

Mon cœur qui dans les nuits parfois cherche à s'entendre
Ou de quel dernier mot t'appeler le plus tendre
S'exalte en celui rien que chuchoté de sœur

N'était, très grand trésor et tête si petite,
Que tu m'enseignes bien toute une autre douceur
Tout bas par le baiser seul dans tes cheveux dite.

So dear far off and near and white, so
deliciously you, Méry, that I dream
of some rare balm emanated by falsehood
on a darkened crystal vase.

You know, for me, for years now, always
your dazzling smile has prolonged
the one rose whose summer plunges
into the past and then back into the future.

My heart that at night sometimes seeks to be heard
or for what most tender, final word to call you
rejoices in none of these but in murmuring *sister*

were it not, great treasure and head so small,
that you teach me an entirely other mildness
by the one kiss spoken lightly in your hair.

Rien, au réveil, que vous n'ayez
Envisagé de quelque moue
Pire si le rire secoue
Votre aile sur les oreillers.

Indifféremment sommeillez
Sans crainte qu'une haleine avoue
Rien, au réveil, que vous n'ayez
Envisagé de quelque moue.

Tous les rêves émerveillés,
Quand cette beauté les déjoue,
Ne produisent fleur sur la joue
Dans l'œil diamants impayés
Rien, au réveil, que vous n'ayez.

Nothing, on waking, you won't have
envisaged with a pout
or worse if laughter shake
your wing on the pillow.

Sleep indifferently
with no fear that a breath might confess
something, on waking, you won't have
envisaged with a pout.

All the dreams filled with wonder,
when this beauty eludes them,
won't bring a rose to the cheek
in the eye unpaid diamonds
nothing you won't have, on waking.

Si tu veux nous nous aimerons
Avec tes lèvres sans le dire
Cette rose ne l'interromps
Qu'à verser un silence pire

Jamais de chants ne lancent prompts
Le scintillement du sourire
Si tu veux nous nous aimerons
Avec tes lèvres sans le dire

Muet muet entre les ronds
Sylphe dans la pourpre d'empire
Un baiser flambant se déchire
Jusqu'aux pointes des ailerons
Si tu veux nous nous aimerons.

If you want us to make love
with your lips don't say so
or interrupt this rose
you'll only make the silence worse

a song never prompted
the scintillation of a smile
if you want us to make love
with your lips don't say so

mute mute between repeats
sylph in imperial purple
a kiss will burst in flames
to its very wingtips
if you want us to make love.

Hors de la poix rien à faire,
Le lis naît blanc, comme odeur
Simplement je le préfère
A ce bon raccommodeur.

Il va de cuir à ma paire
Adjoindre plus que je n'eus
Jamais, cela désespère
Un besoin de talons nus

Son marteau qui ne dévie
Fixe de clous gouailleurs
Sur la semelle l'envie
Toujours conduisant ailleurs.

Il recréerait nos souliers,
O pieds, si vous le vouliez!

Le Carreleur de Souliers

Chansons bas

I

(le Savetier)

Hors de la poix rien à faire,
Le lys naît blanc, comme odeur
Simplement je le préfère
À ce bon raccommodeur.

Il va de cuir à ma paire
Adjoindre plus que je n'eus
Jamais, cela désespère
Un besoin de talons nus.

Son marteau qui ne dévie
Fixe de clous gouailleurs
Sur la semelle l'envie
Toujours conduisant ailleurs.

Il recréerait des souliers,
Ô pieds, si vous le vouliez!

Low Songs

I

(The Cobbler)

Out of tar, what can you do,
the lily is born white, and for
odour simply I prefer
it to this good mender.

He's going to add more leather
to my pair than ever I
had, this drives a need
of naked heels to despair.

His hammer does not miss a blow
to fix with taunting tacks
on the sole the itch
conducting the soul elsewhere.

He would recreate shoes
from scratch, if you wanted, feet!

Cypes de la Rue

La petite Marchande de Lavandes

Ta paille azur de lavandes,
Ne crois pas avec ce cil
Osé que tu me la vendes
Comme à l'hypocrite s'il

En décore la faïence
Où chacun jamais complet
Tapi dans sa défaillance
Au bleu sentiment se plait :

Mieux entre une envahissante
Chevelure ici mets-la
Que le brin salubre y sente,
Zéphyrine, Paméla

Pour décerner à l'époux
Les prémices de tes poux.

27

136

II

(la Marchande
d'herbes aromatiques)

Ta paille azur de lavandes,
Ne crois pas avec ce cil
Osé que tu me la vendes
Comme à l'hypocrite s'il

En tapisse la muraille
De lieux les absolus lieux
Pour le ventre qui se raille
Renaître aux sentiments bleus.

Mieux entre une envahissante
Chevelure ici mets-la
Que le brin salubre y sente,
Zéphirine, Paméla

Ou conduise vers l'époux
Les prémices de tes poux.

II

(The Seller of
Aromatic Herbs)

Don't believe that with a bold
eyelash you will sell me
your blue lavender straw
as to a hypocrite who

hangs it on the wall
of the place the absolute place
for the belly that scoffs
to be reborn in blue sentiments

better to put it here
in a grown-out hairdo
that the salubrious sprig might scent
Pamela, like a Zephyr

or conduct to your spouse
the first-born of your lice.

Le Cantonnier

Ces cailloux, tu les nivelles,
Et c'est, comme troubadour,
Un cube aussi de cervelles
Qu'il me faut ouvrir par jour.

III

(le Cantonnier)

Ces cailloux, tu les nivelles
Et c'est, comme troubadour,
Un cube aussi de cervelles
Qu'il me faut ouvrir par jour.

III

(The Roadmender)

You level these cobbles
and there is, as a troubadour,
a block of brains I too
must open up per day.

Le Marchand d'ail
et
d'oignons

L'ENNUI d'aller en visite
Avec l'ail nous l'éloignons.
L'élégie au pleur hésite
Peu si je fends des oignons.

IV

*(le Marchand d'ail et
d'oignons)*

L'ennui d'aller en visite
Avec l'ail nous l'éloignons.
L'élégie au pleur hésite
Peu si je fends des oignons.

IV

*(The Seller of Garlic
and Onions)*

With garlic we keep at bay
the boredom of the social round.
The tearful elegy is not slow
coming if I chop onions.

La femme du Carrier

La femme, l'enfant, la soupe
En chemin pour le carrier
Le complimentent qu'il coupe
Dans l'us de se marier.

V

(la Femme de l'ouvrier)

La femme, l'enfant, la soupe
En chemin pour le carrier
Le complimentent qu'il coupe
Dans l'us de se marier.

V

(The Worker's Wife)

The wife, the child, the soup
on the way to the quarryman
compliment him on cutting
into the custom of marrying.

VI

(le Vitrier)

Le pur soleil qui remise
Trop d'éclat pour l'y trier
Ôte ébloui sa chemise
Sur le dos du vitrier.

VI

(The Glazier)

The pure sun that sheds
too great a glare to discern it there,
dazzled, takes off his shirt
on the glazier's back.

Toujours, n'importe le titre,
Sans même s'enrhumer au
Dégel, ce gai siffle-litre
Crie un premier numéro.

Le Crieur d'imprimés

28

VII

(le Crieur d'imprimés)

Toujours, n'importe le titre,
Sans même s'enrhumer au
Dégel, ce gai siffle-litre
Crie un premier numéro.

VII

(The Newspaper Seller)

Always, no matter what headline,
without even catching cold in the
thaw, this cheerful guzzler of pints
cries a first edition.

La Marchande
d'habits

LE vif œil dont tu regardes
Jusques à leur contenu
Me sépare de mes hardes,
Et comme un dieu je vais nu.

Stéphane Mallarmé

VIII

*(la Marchande
d'habits)*

Le vif œil dont tu regardes
Jusques à leur contenu
Me sépare de mes hardes
Et comme un dieu je vais nu.

VIII

*(The Seller of Old
Clothes)*

The keen eye by which you look
all the way in to their contents
separates me from my rags
and like a god I go naked.

Billet

Pas les rafales à propos
De rien comme occuper la rue
Sujette au noir vol de chapeaux;
Mais une danseuse apparue

Tourbillon de mousseline ou
Fureur éparses en écumes
Que soulève par son genou
Celle même dont nous vécûmes

Pour tout, hormis lui, rebattu
Spirituelle, ivre, immobile
Foudroyer avec le tutu,
Sans se faire autrement de bile

Sinon rieur que puisse l'air
De sa jupe éventer Whistler.

Note

Not such gusts of wind to no purpose
as occupy the street
subject to the black flight of hats;
but a dancer arisen

the one we all lived for
whirlwind of muslin or
fury dispersed in foam
which she lifts with one knee

to strike everything hackneyed — except
him — with the lightning of a tutu,
spirited, drunk, immobile
venting no other bile

except to laugh that this old air
from her skirt might fan Whistler.

Petit air

I

Quelconque une solitude
Sans le cygne ni le quai
Mire sa désuétude
Au regard que j'abdiquai

Ici de la gloriole
Haute à ne la pas toucher
Dont maint ciel se bariole
Avec les ors de coucher

Mais langoureusement longe
Comme de blanc linge ôté
Tel fugace oiseau si plonge
Exultatrice à côté

Dans l'onde toi devenue
Ta jubilation nue

Little Tune

I

Any given solitude
with neither swan nor quayside
mirrors its obsolescence
in the gaze I abdicated

here from the vain glory
too high to be touched
in which many a dappled sky
puts on sunset gold

but languorously follows
like white linen cast off
some ephemeral bird if plunges
adjacent exultatrix

into the wave become you
your nude jubilation

Petit air

II

Indomptablement a dû
Comme mon espoir s'y lance
Éclater là-haut perdu
Avec furie et silence,

Voix étrangère au bosquet
Ou par nul écho suivie,
L'oiseau qu'on n'ouït jamais
Une autre fois en la vie.

Le hagard musicien,
Cela dans le doute expire
Si de mon sein pas du sien
A jailli le sanglot pire

Déchiré va-t-il entier
Rester sur quelque sentier!

Little Tune

II

Indomitably must
like my far-flung hopes
have gone up with a bang, lost
in fury and silence,

voice stranger to the wood
or followed by no echo,
the bird you get to hear
only once.

The haggard musician,
expiring in doubt
that my breast and not his
might have issued the louder sob

blown apart will all of him
still hit the road!

Petit air

(Guerrier)

Ce me va hormis l'y taire
Que je sente du foyer
Un pantalon militaire
À ma jambe rougeoyer

L'invasion je la guette
Avec le vierge courroux
Tout juste de la baguette
Au gant blanc des tourlourous

Nue ou d'écorce tenace
Pas pour battre le Teuton
Mais comme une autre menace
À la fin que me veut-on

De trancher ras cette ortie
Folle de la sympathie

Little Tune

(Warlike)

I can't not say
I sense from my fireside
military trousers
their scarlet glow on my leg

I await the invasion
with just the virgin
wrath of the baton
in the soldier's white glove

bare or still covered in bark
not to batter the Teuton
but as another threat
to the end expected in me

to cut short this wild
nettle of sympathy

PLUSIEURS SONNETS

Quand l'ombre menaça de la fatale loi
Tel vieux Rêve, désir et mal de mes vertèbres,
Affligé de périr sous les plafonds funèbres
Il a ployé son aile indubitable en moi.

Luxe, ô salle d'ébène où, pour séduire un roi
Se tordent dans leur mort des guirlandes célèbres,
Vous n'êtes qu'un orgueil menti par les ténèbres
Aux yeux du solitaire ébloui de sa foi.

Oui, je sais qu'au lointain de cette nuit, la Terre
Jette d'un grand éclat l'insolite mystère,
Sous les siècles hideux qui l'obscurcissent moins.

L'espace à soi pareil qu'il s'accroisse ou se nie
Roule dans cet ennui des feux vils pour témoins
Que s'est d'un astre en fête allumé le génie.

SEVERAL SONNETS

When the shadow threatened with unalterable law
that old Dream, desire and pain of my spinal column,
afflicted with dying beneath funereal ceilings
it folded its undoubted wing in me.

Luxury, O ebony hall where, to enchant a king,
celebrated garlands writhe in death,
you are only pride, a lie the darkness tells
to the eyes of the hermit dazzled by his faith.

Yes, I know that, on the backdrop of this night, the Earth
projects the unwonted mystery of brilliance
under hideous centuries which obscure it less.

Space, self-identical, if it inflate or deny itself
rolls out cheap fires in this boredom as witness
that genius has ignited in a festive star.

Le vierge, le vivace et le bel aujourd'hui
Va-t-il nous déchirer avec un coup d'aile ivre
Ce lac dur oublié que hante sous le givre
Le transparent glacier des vols qui n'ont pas fui!

Un cygne d'autrefois se souvient que c'est lui
Magnifique mais qui sans espoir se délivre
Pour n'avoir pas chanté la région où vivre
Quand du stérile hiver a resplendi l'ennui.

Tout son col secouera cette blanche agonie
Par l'espace infligée à l'oiseau qui le nie,
Mais non l'horreur du sol où le plumage est pris.

Fantôme qu'à ce lieu son pur éclat assigne,
Il s'immobilise au songe froid de mépris
Que vêt parmi l'exil inutile le Cygne.

The virginal, enduring, beautiful today
will a drunken beat of its wing break us
this hard, forgotten lake haunted under frost
by the transparent glacier of unfled flights!

A swan of old remembers it is he
magnificent but who without hope frees himself
for never having sung a place to live
when the boredom of sterile winter was resplendent.

His whole neck will shake off this white death-throe
inflicted by space on the bird denying it,
but not the horror of soil where the feathers are caught.

Phantom assigned to this place by pure brilliance,
he is paralysed in the cold dream of contempt
put on in useless exile by the Swan.

Victorieusement fui le suicide beau
Tison de gloire, sang par écume, or, tempête!
Ô rire si là-bas une pourpre s'apprête
À ne tendre royal que mon absent tombeau.

Quoi! de tout cet éclat pas même le lambeau
S'attarde, il est minuit, à l'ombre qui nous fête
Excepté qu'un trésor présomptueux de tête
Verse son caressé nonchaloir sans flambeau,

La tienne si toujours le délice! la tienne
Oui seule qui du ciel évanoui retienne
Un peu de puéril triomphe en t'en coiffant

Avec clarté quand sur les coussins tu la poses
Comme un casque guerrier d'impératrice enfant
Dont pour te figurer il tomberait des roses.

In victory having fled fair suicide
a brand of glory, blood in foam, gold, tempest!
what a laugh if, down there, a royal purple is pressed
for nothing but to drape my absent tomb.

Not one scrap of all that brilliance lingers,
it is midnight, in the shade that celebrates us,
except the presumptuous treasure of a head
that pours its pampered nonchalance in darkness,

yours, always a delight! yes, yours alone
that holds back from the vanished sky a bit
of puerile triumph, doing up your hair

with light as you compose it on the cushions
like the battle helmet of an infant empress
from which, to stand for you, would tumble roses.

Ses purs ongles très haut dédiant leur onyx,
L'Angoisse ce minuit, soutient, lampadophore,
Maint rêve vespéral brûlé par le Phénix
Que ne recueille pas de cinéraire amphore

Sur les crédences, au salon vide: nul ptyx,
Aboli bibelot d'inanité sonore,
(Car le Maître est allé puiser des pleurs au Styx
Avec ce seul objet dont le Néant s'honore.)

Mais proche la croisée au nord vacante, un or
Agonise selon peut-être le décor
Des licornes ruant du feu contre une nixe,

Elle, défunte nue en le miroir, encor
Que, dans l'oubli fermé par le cadre, se fixe
De scintillations sitôt le septuor.

Its pure nails raised to consecrate their onyx,
Anguish, this midnight, holds up, lampadephore,
many a vesperal dream burned by the Phoenix
that is gathered in no cinerary amphora

on the credences, in the empty salon: no ptyx,
abolished bauble inanely echoing,
(for the Master has gone to draw tears from the Styx
with this one object on which Nothing prides itself).

But near the cross-pane vacant to the north, a gold
is dying, perhaps in sympathy with the décor
of unicorns kicking fire against a nixe,

she, defunct nude in the mirror, even
though, in oblivion closed by the frame, at once
the septet of fixed scintillations settles.

Sonnet

2 novembre 1877

— « Sur les bois oubliés quand passe l'hiver sombre
Tu te plains, ô captif solitaire du seuil,
Que ce sépulcre à deux qui fera notre orgueil
Hélas! du manque seul des lourds bouquets s'encombre.

Sans écouter Minuit qui jeta son vain nombre,
Une veille t'exalte à ne pas fermer l'œil
Avant que dans les bras de l'ancien fauteuil
Le suprême tison n'ait éclairé mon Ombre.

Qui veut souvent avoir la Visite ne doit
Par trop de fleurs charger la pierre que mon doigt
Soulève avec l'ennui d'une force défunte.

Âme au si clair foyer tremblante de m'asseoir,
Pour revivre il suffit qu'à tes lèvres j'emprunte
Le souffle de mon nom murmuré tout un soir. »

(Pour votre chère morte, son ami.)

Sonnet

2 November 1877

— "When sombre winter sweeps forgotten woods
you complain, o solitary captive of the threshold,
that this twin sepulchre our pride to be
is burdened by the lack of heavy flowers.

Not hearing Midnight tolling its vain number,
a vigil stirs you not to close an eye
till, in the safe arms of an antique chair
my Shade's revealed by a persisting ember.

If you would have the Visit often, don't
load with too many flowers the stone my finger
lifts with the boredom of a defunct force.

Soul trembling to sit down by such a hearth,
to live I need to borrow from your lips
only my name's breath murmured until nightfall."

(For your dear dead one, her friend.)

Le Tombeau d'Edgar Poe

Tel qu'en Lui-même enfin l'éternité le change,
Le Poëte suscite avec un glaive nu
Son siècle épouvanté de n'avoir pas connu
Que la mort triomphait dans cette voix étrange!

Eux, comme un vil sursaut d'hydre oyant jadis l'ange
Donner un sens plus pur aux mots de la tribu
Proclamèrent très haut le sortilège bu
Dans le flot sans honneur de quelque noir mélange.

Du sol et de la nue hostiles, ô grief!
Si notre idée avec ne sculpte un bas-relief
Dont la tombe de Poe éblouissante s'orne

Calme bloc ici-bas chu d'un désastre obscur
Que ce granit du moins montre à jamais sa borne
Aux noirs vols du Blasphème épars dans le futur.

The Tomb of Edgar Poe

Such as into Himself at last eternity changes him,
the Poet with a naked sword provokes
his century appalled to not have known
death triumphed in that strange voice!

They, like an upstart hydra hearing the angel once
purify the meaning of tribal words
proclaimed out loud the prophecy drunk
without honour in the tide of some black mixture.

From soil and hostile cloud, what strife!
if our idea fails to sculpt a bas-relief
to ornament the dazzling tomb of Poe,

calm block fallen down here from an unseen disaster,
let this granite at least set for all time a limit
to the black flights of Blasphemy scattered in the future.

Le Tombeau de Charles Baudelaire

Le temple enseveli divulgue par la bouche
Sépulcrale d'égout bavant boue et rubis
Abominablement quelque idole Anubis
Tout le museau flambé comme un aboi farouche

Ou que le gaz récent torde la mèche louche
Essuyeuse on le sait des opprobres subis
Il allume hagard un immortel pubis
Dont le vol selon le réverbère découche

Quel feuillage séché dans les cités sans soir
Votif pourra bénir comme elle se rasseoir
Contre le marbre vainement de Baudelaire

Au voile qui la ceint absente avec frissons
Celle son Ombre même un poison tutélaire
Toujours à respirer si nous en périssons

The Tomb of Charles Baudelaire

The buried temple via the horribly dribbling
sepulchral sewer-mouth loosening mud and rubies
divulges a kind of idol of Anubis
the whole muzzle fired up like a savage bark

if recent gas screws up the shiftless wick
well-known assuager of endured disgrace
it lights up wildly an immortal pubis
kept up all night in flight by the street-lamp

what votive foliage dried in the duskless cities
will bless like she does as she sits back vainly
down on the marble lid of Baudelaire

absent and shivering in the veil that girds her
being his Shade a tutelary poison
we breathe in deeply though we die of it

Tombeau

Anniversaire — Janvier 1897

Le noir roc courroucé que la bise le roule
Ne s'arrêtera ni sous de pieuses mains
Tâtant sa ressemblance avec les maux humains
Comme pour en bénir quelque funeste moule.

Ici presque toujours si le ramier roucoule
Cet immatériel deuil opprime de maints
Nubiles plis l'astre mûri des lendemains
Dont un scintillement argentera la foule.

Qui cherche, parcourant le solitaire bond
Tantôt extérieur de notre vagabond —
Verlaine? Il est caché parmi l'herbe, Verlaine

À ne surprendre que naïvement d'accord
La lèvre sans y boire ou tarir son haleine
Un peu profond ruisseau calomnié la mort.

Tomb

Anniversary — January 1897

The black rock raging that the North Wind rolls it
will not be arrested even by pious hands
testing its resemblance to human suffering
as if to bless some fatal cast of it.

Here almost always if the ring dove coos
this immaterial mourning oppresses with many
nubile folds the future ripened star
whose scintillation will silverplate the crowd.

Who seeks, shadowing the solitary leap
only just now external of our vagabond —
Verlaine? He is hidden in the grass, Verlaine

to surprise, but only naively in agreement,
the lip not drinking there and withholding breath,
a shallow stream defamed by the name death.

Hommage

Le silence déjà funèbre d'une moire
Dispose plus qu'un pli seul sur le mobilier
Que doit un tassement du principal pilier
Précipiter avec le manque de mémoire.

Notre si vieil ébat triomphal du grimoire,
Hiéroglyphes dont s'exalte le millier
À propager de l'aile un frisson familier!
Enfouissez-le-moi plutôt dans une armoire.

Du souriant fracas originel haï
Entre elles de clartés maîtresses a jailli
Jusque vers un parvis né pour leur simulacre,

Trompettes tout haut d'or pâmé sur les vélins,
Le dieu Richard Wagner irradiant un sacre
Mal tu par l'encre même en sanglots sibyllins.

Homage

The already funereal silence of a silk
arranges more than one fold on the furniture
a subsidence of the central pillar must
throw down with default of memory.

Our so old triumphal frolic of the grammar,
hieroglyphs the multitude exalts in
to spread with a wing the familiar shiver!
Bury it for me rather in a cupboard.

From the original smiling uproar hated
among them, of master clarities, has burst
as far as a parvis born for their simulacrum,

gold trumpets swooning out loud on vellum,
the god Richard Wagner irradiating a sacrament
unmuted even by ink in sibylline sobs.

Hommage

Toute Aurore même gourde
À crisper un poing obscur
Contre des clairons d'azur
Embouchés par cette sourde

A le pâtre avec la gourde
Jointe au bâton frappant dur
Le long de son pas futur
Tant que la source ample sourde

Par avance ainsi tu vis
Ô solitaire Puvis
De Chavannes
                        jamais seul

De conduire le temps boire
À la nymphe sans linceul
Que lui découvre ta Gloire

Homage

Every Dawn even so numb
as to clench a dark fist
against blue clarions
sounded by her in deafness

has a shepherd with a gourd
joined to a stick striking hard
alongside his future footstep
that an ample spring might rise

so by advance you live
O solitary Puvis
de Chavannes
                    never alone

in leading our time to drink
at the nymph in no shroud
your Glory discovers to it

Au seul souci de voyager
Outre une Inde splendide et trouble
— Ce salut va, le messager
Du temps, cap que ta poupe double

Comme sur quelque vergue bas
Plongeante avec la caravelle
Écumait toujours en ébats
Un oiseau d'ivresse nouvelle

Qui criait monotonement
Sans que la barre ne varie
Un inutile gisement
Nuit, désespoir et pierrerie

Par son chant reflété jusqu'au
Sourire du pâle Vasco.

To the one concern of voyaging
beyond splendid troubled Indies
— this greeting goes, the messenger
of time, cape your poop rounds

as upon some low yardarm
plunging with the caravel
a bird of new drunkenness
frolicked in foam

and cried on one note
though the tiller never varied
a useless bearing
night, despair and gemstone

reflected by its song as far
as pale Vasco's smile.

Toute l'âme résumée
Quand lente nous l'expirons
Dans plusieurs ronds de fumée
Abolis en autres ronds

Atteste quelque cigare
Brûlant savamment pour peu
Que la cendre se sépare
De son clair baiser de feu

Ainsi le chœur des romances
À la lèvre vole-t-il
Exclus-en si tu commences
Le réel parce que vil

Le sens trop précis rature
Ta vague littérature

All soul summed up
when slowly we exhale it
in plural rings of smoke
revoked by other rings

attests some cigar
burning skilfully so long
as the ash uncouples
from its bright kiss of fire

if thus the chorus
of love-songs leaps to your lip
exclude from it to begin with
the real   it is cheap

too precise sense scores out
your vague literature

I

Tout Orgueil fume-t-il du soir,
Torche dans un branle étouffée
Sans que l'immortelle bouffée
Ne puisse à l'abandon surseoir!

La chambre ancienne de l'hoir
De maint riche mais chu trophée
Ne serait pas même chauffée
S'il survenait par le couloir.

Affres du passé nécessaires
Agrippant comme avec des serres
Le sépulcre de désaveu,

Sous un marbre lourd qu'elle isole
Ne s'allume pas d'autre feu
Que la fulgurante console.

I

Does all Pride smoke of an evening,
torch snuffed out in a jerk,
the immortal puff with no power
to postpone the surrender!

The former chamber of the heir
to many a rich but fallen trophy
would not even be warmed
if he came back in through the hall.

Necessary terrors of the past
clutching as if with claws
at the tomb of denial,

under heavy marble which it isolates
no other fire ignites
than the star-struck console.

II

Surgi de la croupe et du bond
D'une verrerie éphémère
Sans fleurir la veillée amère
Le col ignoré s'interrompt.

Je crois bien que deux bouches n'ont
Bu, ni son amant ni ma mère,
Jamais à la même Chimère,
Moi, sylphe de ce froid plafond!

Le pur vase d'aucun breuvage
Que l'inexhaustible veuvage
Agonise mais ne consent,

Naïf baiser des plus funèbres!
À rien expirer annonçant
Une rose dans les ténèbres.

II

Arisen from the aspirant rump
of ephemeral glassware
rather than garlanding the bitter vigil
the neck breaks off, ignored.

I well believe two mouths never
drank, not her lover, not my mother,
not from the one Chimera,
I, sylph of this cold ceiling!

The vessel, pure of any fluid
but everlasting widowhood,
in dying does not consent,

naïve, most funereal kiss!
on an out-breath to announce
a rose in darkness.

III

Une dentelle s'abolit
Dans le doute du Jeu suprême
À n'entr'ouvrir comme un blasphème
Qu'absence éternelle de lit.

Cet unanime blanc conflit
D'une guirlande avec la même,
Enfui contre la vitre blême
Flotte plus qu'il n'ensevelit.

Mais, chez qui du rêve se dore
Tristement dort une mandore
Au creux néant musicien

Telle que vers quelque fenêtre
Selon nul ventre que le sien,
Filial on aurait pu naître.

III

Lace cancels itself out
in doubt of the supreme Game
to half-reveal like a blasphemy   only
eternal absence of bed.

This unanimous white conflict
of a garland with the same,
rushing against the pale glass
floats more than it shrouds.

But, in him who is bronzed by the dream
sadly there sleeps a mandola
in the hollow   musician-like nothing

such that towards some window,
by means of no womb but its own,
filial, one might have been born.

Quelle soie aux baumes de temps
Où la Chimère s'exténue
Vaut la torse et native nue
Que, hors de ton miroir, tu tends!

Les trous de drapeaux méditants
S'exaltent dans une avenue:
Moi, j'ai ta chevelure nue
Pour enfouir des yeux contents.

Non. La bouche ne sera sûre
De rien goûter à sa morsure,
S'il ne fait, ton princier amant,

Dans la considérable touffe
Expirer, comme un diamant,
Le cri des Gloires qu'il étouffe.

What silk, embalmed by time
where the Chimera wore off
is worth the twisted, native cloud
you stretch beyond your mirror!

The holes of meditating flags
are raised in an avenue —
me, I have your undressed hair
to bury happy eyes in.

No. The biting mouth will not
be sure of tasting anything
if your princely lover does not make

the cry of Glory he stifles
expire, like a diamond
in the considerable tuft.

M'introduire dans ton histoire
C'est en héros effarouché
S'il a du talon nu touché
Quelque gazon de territoire

À des glaciers attentatoire
Je ne sais le naïf péché
Que tu n'auras pas empêché
De rire très haut sa victoire

Dis si je ne suis pas joyeux
Tonnerre et rubis aux moyeux
De voir en l'air que ce feu troue

Avec des royaumes épars
Comme mourir pourpre la roue
Du seul vespéral de mes chars

To insert myself into your plot
it's as a hero alarmed
if he has touched with naked heel
some territorial lawn

I do not know the naïve sin
destructive to glaciers
you would not have prevented
from laughing out loud its victory

tell me if I am not glad
thunder and rubies at the hub
to see in the air this fire holes

with scattered kingdoms
the wheel of my one vesperal car
as if dying in purple

À la nue accablante tu
Basse de basalte et de laves
À même les échos esclaves
Par une trompe sans vertu

Quel sépulcral naufrage (tu
Le sais, écume, mais y baves)
Suprême une entre les épaves
Abolit le mât dévêtu

Ou cela que furibond faute
De quelque perdition haute
Tout l'abîme vain éployé

Dans le si blanc cheveu qui traîne
Avarement aura noyé
Le flanc enfant d'une sirène

Struck dumb at the cloud-base
lowering basalt and lava
on top of enslaved echoes
by a worthless horn

what sepulchral shipwreck (you
know it, foam, but just drivel)
supreme among flotsam
stripped the mast bare, then annulled it

or the one that, mad for the want
of some fine distress
the abyss spread uselessly

in a single bright white hair
will have drowned like a miser
the flank of a siren child

Mes bouquins refermés sur le nom de Paphos,
Il m'amuse d'élire avec le seul génie
Une ruine, par mille écumes bénie
Sous l'hyacinthe, au loin, de ses jours triomphaux.

Coure le froid avec ses silences de faulx,
Je n'y hululerai pas de vide nénie
Si ce très blanc ébat au ras du sol dénie
À tout site l'honneur du paysage faux.

Ma faim qui d'aucuns fruits ici ne se régale
Trouve en leur docte manque une saveur égale:
Qu'un éclate de chair humain et parfumant!

Le pied sur quelque guivre où notre amour tisonne,
Je pense plus longtemps peut-être éperdûment
À l'autre, au sein brûlé d'une antique amazone.

My old books closed again on the name Paphos,
it amuses me with my one talent to choose
a ruin, blessed by a thousand flecks of foam
under the distant hyacinth of its heyday.

Let the cold pour its scything silences,
I will hoot no empty keening
if this white frolic on the soil deny
to all loci the honour of the false landscape.

My hunger, treating itself to no fruits here
finds in their learned lack an equal savour:
let one burst out in fragrant, human flesh!

My foot on some wyvern where our love stirs the coals,
I think far longer, perhaps in desperation
of the other, burned breast of an antique amazon.

BIBLIOGRAPHY[1]

This First Notebook, except for the insertion of a few pieces jotted down rather as decorations in the margins

> Salut
> Éventail, de Madame Mallarmé
> Feuillet d'Album
> Remémoration, d'Amis Belges
> Chansons Bas I and II
> Billet, à Whistler
> Petit air I and II,

and the Sonnets

> le Tombeau de Charles Baudelaire
> "À la nue accablante tu"

follows the order, without the grouping, presented by the facsimile Edition of the author's manuscript, published in 1887.

Apart from some corrections, introduced with the reprinting of the Selected Works, *Vers et Prose*, by the Librairie Académique, the text remains that of the beautiful subscription publication which fixed it (and then took flight in so many auction rooms). Its rarity was already garlanded, in the original format, with the masterpiece by Rops.

No earlier readings are given here, as variants.

Many of these poems, or studies in view of something better, as one might try out the nib of a pen before settling down to work, were abstracted from their files by the friendly impatiences of Magazines looking to produce their first number: and they form a record of projects, as defining points of reference, too rare or too numerous, according to the double point of view which the

---

[1] This is a translation of Mallarmé's own bibliographical note, prepared for the edition of the *Poésies* which was published posthumously in 1899.

author himself shares; he preserves them for the reason that Youth wanted to take some account of them, and to create a Public around them.

Salut (page 8): this Sonnet, recently, while raising the glass, at a Banquet of *la Plume*, along with the honour of presiding there.

Apparition (page 18) tempted musicians, among them MM. Bailly and André Rossignol who adapted delicious notes to it.

Le Pitre châtié (page 22) appeared for the first time, already old, in the great edition of *la Revue Indépendante*.

Les Fenêtres, Les Fleurs, Renouveau, Angoisse (at first called *À Celle qui est tranquille*), *Le Sonneur, Tristesse d'été, L'Azur, Brise marine, Soupir, Aumône* (entitled *le Mendiant*), *"Las de l'amer repos où ma paresse offense"* (pages 26 to 57) make up the series which, in this still-cited work, is called the *Premier Parnasse contemporain*.

Hérodiade (page 68), here a fragment, or only the part in dialogue, comprises, in addition to the cantique de saint Jean and its conclusion in a final monologue, a Prelude and Finale which will be published later, and turn out to be a poem.

L'Après-midi d'un faune (page 90) appeared separately, interiorly-decorated by Manet, one of the first expensive pamphlets, made up like a bag of sweets but perfect and a little oriental with its "Japanese felt, title in gold and tied with black and rose-de-Chine cords" as the brochure puts it: then M. Dujardin made, of these verses which were impossible to find except in his photogravure, a popular edition, which is out of print.

Toast Funèbre comes from the collective publication *le Tombeau de Théophile Gautier*, Master and Shade to whom the invocation is addressed: his name appears, in rhyme, before the end.

Prose pour des Esseintes; he might, perhaps, have inserted it, just as it appears on page 110, in the *À Rebours* of our own Huysmans.

"Tout à coup et comme par jeu" is copied indiscreetly from the album of the

daughter of the provençal poet Roumanille, my old comrade: I admired her as a child and when she was a young lady she wanted to ask me for some verses, to remind her of it.

Remémoration.. — I had the pleasure of sending this sonnet to the Visitor's Book of the Cercle Excelsior, where I gave a lecture and made friends.

Chansons Bas I and *II*, along with various quatrains, comment upon the illustrations in the collection *Les Types de Paris*, by the Master-Painter Raffaelli, who inspired them and accepted them.

Billet appeared, in French, as an illustration in the English journal *the Whirlwind*, towards which Whistler was generous as a prince.

Petits airs, I, to inaugurate, November 1894, the magnificent publication *L'Épreuve*. *II*. belongs to the album of M. Daudet.

Le Tombeau d'Edgar Poe — it was recited as part of the ceremony, at the erecting of a monument to Poe, in Baltimore, a block of basalt placed by America upon the nimble shade of the poet, for its own safety, to make sure that it never got back out again.

Le Tombeau de Charles Baudelaire — formed part of the book having this title, published by subscription with a view to creating some statue, bust or commemorative medallion.

Hommage, among others, of a French poet, solicited by the admirable *Revue Wagnérienne*, which vanished with the definitive triumph of the Genius.

So much attention to detail bears witness, uselessly perhaps, to some deference to future scholiasts.

SCHOLIA[2]

Salut (page 8)

Spoken by Mallarmé as a toast at a banquet held by the journal *La Plume*, and published (under the title 'Toast') in that journal on 15th February 1893.

Title: "Salut" can mean "a state of salvation" as well as an informal salutation (hello, goodbye, or "cheers!", depending on the context). The ambiguity is also active in the last word of Mallarmé's 'Cantique de saint Jean'.

L. 1 — *Rien*: the association between beginning and negation is native to any language, like French or English, which inherits the Greek prefix "privative a", used in words like "atypical" and "atheist" ("Alpha being chosen as queen of the alphabet because she meant 'not'").[3]

L. 1 — *cette écume*: compare the ending of Anna Laetitia Barbauld's poem 'Washing-Day' (1797):

> Earth, air, and sky, and ocean, hath its bubbles,
> And verse is one of them — this most of all.

L. 1-2 — *vierge vers ... la coupe*: Roger Pearson[4] notes the presence of two constellations, Virgo (The Virgin) and Crater (The Cup). These constellations are located next to one another on the celestial equator, and are presumably the star(s) by which the poet and his friends navigate. "Vers" puns on "verre" ("a drinking-glass") and "coupe" on the French word for a metrical caesura.

L. 3 — *se noie*: given the context, perhaps an echo of the expression "se noyer dans un verre d'eau" ("to drown in a glass of water; to be lost for the slightest of reasons").

---

[2] *Scolie* (n.f.): 1. A grammatical or critical note to aid the interpretation of classical authors. 2. Among the ancient Greeks, a drinking-song (Littré).
[3] Jack Spicer, 'Language' (in *My vocabulary did this to me*, 395).
[4] *Mallarmé and Circumstance*, 243.

L. 5 — *divers*: with a pun on the English plural noun[5] (this is supported by 'L'Après-midi d'un faune', line 62ff., where the "SOUVENIRS divers" are similarly associated with the verb "noyer").

L. 6 — *la poupe*: the Ptolemaic southern constellation Argo Navis (The Ship Argo) was divided (by Lacaille, 1752) into three smaller constellations, Puppis (The Poop), Carina (The Keel) and Vela (The Sails), a division which was in itself a kind of shipwreck. In the *Argonautica* of Apollonius Rhodius, the Argonauts survive an encounter with the sirens with the help of Orpheus, who drowns out their singing with his own music.[6] In some post-Homeric accounts, the sirens were fated to die if someone heard their song and escaped: Hyginus, *Fabulae* CXLI writes "Ulysses proved fatal to [the sirens], for when by his cleverness he passed by the rocks where they dwelt, they threw themselves into the sea." For another drowned siren, see the poem "À la nue accablante tu…"

L. 7 — *avant*: "the bow of a ship", linked to the poem's title by the English meaning of the verb "saluer" ("to take a bow"). Also a suggestion that the poet's friends are now the "avant-garde", while Mallarmé takes a back seat on the poop.

L. 12 — *Solitude, récif, étoile*: compare this trinity, and the similar "Nuit, désespoir et pierrerie" of "Au seul souci de voyager…", with Baudelaire, 'Le Voyage', II:

> Notre âme est un trois-mâts cherchant son Icarie;
> Une voix retentit sur le pont: «Ouvre l'œil!»
> Une voix de la hune, ardente et folle, crie:
> «Amour … gloire … bonheur!» Enfer! c'est un écueil!

("Our soul is a three-master searching for its Icaria; / a voice sings out over the deck: 'Open your eyes!' / A voice from the topmast, ardent and mad, cries: /

[5] Graham Robb, *Unlocking Mallarmé*, 192.
[6] *Argonautica*, Book IV, lines 885ff.

'Love… glory… happiness!' Hell! it's [*or* 'Hell is'] a reef!") The next stanza of the Baudelaire poem has "récif". In *Odyssey* XII, Circe suggests two alternative routes for Odysseus to follow immediately after his encounter with the sirens: one among the Wandering Rocks, the other between Scylla and Charybdis.

Le Guignon (page 10)

Published in a truncated version (lines 1-15) on 15th March 1862 in the journal *L'Artiste*, and in full in one of Verlaine's essays on Mallarmé in the journal *Lutèce* (17-24th November 1883). Revised substantially before being republished in the 1887 *Poésies*. Austin Gill[7] notes that the poem was probably curtailed by the editors of *L'Artiste* (a journal to which Baudelaire often contributed) because it was understood as an attack on Baudelaire's belief in the heroic nature of artistic suffering. The poem borrows its title from a sonnet in Baudelaire's *Les Fleurs du mal*, and its rhyme scheme (and much of its tone) from Théophile Gautier's long poem 'Ténèbres'. Baudelaire's essay 'Edgar Allan Poe, sa vie, et ses œuvres' opens: "In recent times, a poor wretch was brought before our courts of law, whose brow was illustrated by a rare and strange tattoo: *No luck!* He carried thus, above his eyes, his life's label, as a book bears its title, and the interrogation proved that this bizarre placard was cruelly truthful. In the history of literature there are similar destinies, real damnations, — men who bear the word *guignon* ('ill-fortune') written in mysterious characters in the sinuous folds of their brow. The blind Angel of expiation has seized them, and scourges them hard for the edification of others".

L. 6 — *d'irritables ornières*: the echo of the "genus irritabile vatum" ("the irritable race of poets", Horace, *Epistles*, II, 2, 102) is the first hint that the "mendieurs" are poets. Section 4 of Baudelaire's essay 'Notes nouvelles sur Edgar Poe' opens with a translation of section XXII of Poe's 'Fifty Suggestions', on the irritability of poets.

L. 14 — *dans le nu de son glaive*: compare "Le Poëte suscite avec un glaive nu"

---

[7] *The Early Mallarmé*, vol. 2, 186ff.

('Le Tombeau d'Edgar Poe').

L. 21 — *Dérisoires martyrs*: Austin Gill[8] sees an allusion to Baudelaire's preface (first published in October 1861) to Léon Cladel's *Les Martyrs ridicules*, in which the poet attacked the younger generation of bohemians and writers.

L. 24 — *le destin qui les roue*: "rouer" is literally "to break someone upon a wheel" as a form of torture; the context also suggests Fortune's wheel.

L. 34 — *son buccin bizarre*: this whole tercet is very close to the bizarre blown fanfare in the second tercet of 'Aumône' (the only other one of the *Poésies* written in *terza rima*).

L. 36 — *le poing à leur cul*: the rectal trumpet may have been borrowed from the last line of Dante, *Inferno* XXI.

L. 64 — *se pendre au réverbère*: the poet Gérard de Nerval had hanged himself in 1855, not actually from a lamp-post, but from the railings of a lodging-house in la rue de la Vieille Lanterne ("Old Lantern Street").[9] See also the last line of 'Le Sonneur'.

Apparition (page 18)

Written 1863 or 4, but not published until 1883, when it appeared in Verlaine's essay on Mallarmé in the 24-30th November issue of the journal *Lutèce*. The essay was collected in Verlaine's book *Les Poètes maudits* ("The Cursed Poets", 1884).

L. 4 — *De blancs sanglots*: Roger Pearson[10] notes that a "sanglot" is etymologically a "glottal spasm", something more convulsive than a simple sob. The word recurs frequently in Mallarmé's work, and the poet seems in fact to have died of the etymology of "sanglot" on 9th September 1898, "asphyxiated by a sudden contraction of the glottis".[11]

---

[8] *The Early Mallarmé*, vol. 2, 203.
[9] Benn Sowerby, *The Disinherited: The Life of Gérard de Nerval 1808-1855*, 157.
[10] *Mallarme and Circumstance*, 233.
[11] Gordon Millan, *A Throw of the Dice: the Life of Stéphane Mallarmé*, 317.

Placet futile (page 20)

Published in the journal *Le Papillon*, 25th February 1862 (under the title 'Placet'). This was Mallarmé's first published poem, and incorporates a reworking of part of the slightly earlier 'À une petite laveuse blonde' ("To a little blonde laundrymaid"):

> Ô jours dorés des péronnelles,
> Des Dieux, des balcons enjambés,
> Du fard, des mouches, des dentelles,
> Des petits chiens, et des abbés!
>
> Boucher jusqu'aux seins t'eût noyée
> Dans l'argent du cygne onduleux,
> Cachant sous l'aile déployée
> Ton ris de pourpre et tes yeux bleus.

("O gilded days of scatterbrains, / of Gods, of climbed-over balconies, / of make-up, beauty-spots and lace, / of little dogs and of abbés! // Boucher would have plunged you up to the breast / in the silver of the sinuous swan, / hiding beneath the unfolded wing / your crimson smile and your blue eyes").

L. 1 — *Hébé*: Roger Pearson[12] notes the oblique tribute to Olympe Audouard, editor of *Le Papillon*: Hebe was cupbearer to the Olympian gods.

L. 14 — *nommez-nous berger de vos sourires*: compare *Song of Solomon*, 6:6, "Thy teeth [are] as a flock of sheep which go up from the washing, whereof every one beareth twins, and [there is] not one barren among them" (King James version).

Le Pitre châtié (page 22)

First published in the 1887 *Poésies*. Harold J. Smith[13] notes that the theme of

---

[12] *Unfolding Mallarmé*, 28.
[13] 'Mallarme's Faun: Hero or Antihero?', *The Romanic Review*, 64 (March 1973), 111-

the poem is very similar to that of 'L'Après-midi d'un faune': both the clown and the faun are punished for rejecting their art in favour of sensuality.

L. 1 — *lacs*: with a hint of the homonym meaning "a snare", "a lover's knot", "a noose",[14] or (appropriately to the poem's desire for rebirth), "a cord tied by obstetricians round the limbs of a foetus to facilitate a difficult delivery".[15] L.J. Austin[16] notes that the homonym is pronounced [lɑ] and is phonetically impossible before "avec"…

L. 2-3 — *évoquais / Comme plume*: both evoking/summoning up a plume of soot, and evoking the soot as a quill-pen would in writing about it. Also the feather in Hamlet's hat, and an echo of the "feutre à plume" in 'Le Guignon'.

L. 3 — *la suie ignoble des quinquets*: "quinquets" is also slang for "eyes". L.J. Austin[17] finds this an implausible overtone; however the poem ends with an apotheosis of make-up, and soot is one of the main ingredients of the eye make-up *kohl*.

L. 11-12 — *nacre / Rance*: note the anagram.

The earliest version of the poem, dating from 1864, was quite different:

> Pour ses yeux, — pour nager dans ces lacs, dont les quais
> Sont plantés de beaux cils qu'un matin bleu pénètre,
> J'ai, Muse, — moi, ton pitre, — enjambé la fenêtre
> Et fui notre baraque où fument tes quinquets,
>
> Et d'herbes enivré, j'ai plongé comme un traître
> Dans ces lacs défendus, et, quand tu m'appelais,

124, 112.

[14] Noted by, among others, Robert Greer Cohn, *Toward the Poems of Mallarmé*, 38 and Roger Pearson, *Unfolding Mallarmé*, 43 n.8.

[15] Littré, *lacs* 3°.

[16] *Poetic principles and practice*, 164 n.20.

[17] *Poetic principles and practice*, 160 n.14.

Baigné mes membres nus dans l'onde aux blancs galets,
Oubliant mon habit de pitre au tronc d'un hêtre.

Le soleil du matin séchait mon corps nouveau
Et je sentais fraîchir loin de ta tyrannie
La neige des glaciers dans ma chair assainie,

Ne sachant pas, hélas! quand s'en allait sur l'eau
Le suif de mes cheveux et le fard de ma peau,
Muse, que cette crasse était tout le génie!

("For her eyes, — to swim in these lakes, the quays
planted with lashes a fine blue morning pierces,
Muse, I have, — I, your clown, — stepped through the window
and fled our booth where your oil-lamps are smoking

and drunk on grass, like a traitor I have plunged
in these forbidden lakes, and, while you were calling me,
bathed my bare limbs in the wave by the white shingle,
my clown suit unremembered on a beech-tree trunk.

The morning sun was drying my new body
and far from your tyranny I felt the snow
of glaciers cooling in my flesh made pure,

not knowing, alas! that when my hair-oil
and the greasepaint on my skin fell away in the water,
Muse, that this grime was all there was of genius!")[18]

---

[18] A striking difference between the two versions is the much greater prominence of articulated (rather than elided) 'e muet' in the later version: sixteen instances as compared to seven in the earlier. The effect is to lighten, almost aerate, the texture of the alexandrine line, and it's tempting to read the repeated images of perforation in

"Une négresse par le démon secouée…" (page 24)

Written late 1864 or 5, and published under the title 'Les Lèvres roses' in *Le Nouveau Parnasse satyrique du dix-neuvième siècle*, 1866. Mallarmé's original title was 'Image grotesque', which seems to have been changed to 'Les Lèvres roses' by an editor.

This is the only poem to have been included in the 1887 "photolithographic" edition of the *Poésies* (a facsimile of Mallarmé's handwritten manuscript), but not in the trade edition being prepared for publication at the time of Mallarmé's death. The 1887 edition, of which only 47 copies were printed, was published as a series of nine fascicles. "Une négresse…" occupied the whole of the second fascicle, and was "not to be sold separately".[19] Pdf files of this edition, and of *Le Nouveau Parnasse satyrique*, can be downloaded from the Bibliothèque Nationale website, http://gallica.bnf.fr/

L. 3 — *leur robe trouée*: compare the opening of Baudelaire's poem 'À une mendiante rousse' ("To a red-haired beggar-girl"):

> Blanche fille aux cheveux roux,
> Dont la robe par ses trous
> Laisse voir la pauvreté
>   Et la beauté

("Pale red-haired girl, / whose dress's holes / allow a glimpse of poverty / and of beauty"). The Baudelaire is also echoed in Mallarmé's poem 'Haine du pauvre' (quoted in the notes to 'Aumône', below).

L. 7-8 — *Elle darde … Ainsi que quelque langue*: "darder" is the verb for what a snake's tongue does.[20]

---

the later version of the poem as a comment on its newly-ventilated prosody (the "toile" pierced in line 4 is derived from the same Latin root as "text"). See the afterword, page 282, for more on the 'e muet'.

[19] *OC*, 1394.

[20] Noted by F.C. St. Aubyn, *Stéphane Mallarmé*, 26; see Littré, *darder* 2°.

L. 10 — *sur le dos tel un fol éléphant*: according to the *Encyclopédie* of Diderot and d'Alembert, female elephants lie on their back to mate. Mallarmé had read (and may have written a lost review of) his friend Albert Glatigny's book *Les Flèches d'or* ("The Golden Arrows", 1864),[21] which includes the poem 'L'Idiote' ("The Idiot-girl"):

> Couche-toi donc, belle machine
> Au corps superbe et triomphant!
> Courbe devant moi ton échine,
> De même qu'un jeune éléphant.

("Lie down, then, beautiful machine / superb in body and triumphant! / Bow down your spine before me, / just like a young elephant").

L. 13 — *la victime*: Baudelaire's poem 'Femmes damnées: Delphine et Hippolyte' also describes one of the protagonists in a lesbian encounter as a "victime".

L. 16 — *un coquillage marin*: Littré notes that "le cône cordelier" (*Conus fumigatus*, the smoky cone shell) was also known as a "négresse".

Les Fenêtres (page 26)

Written 1863, and published, along with nine other poems by Mallarmé, in *Le Parnasse contemporain* of 12th May 1866.

L. 1ff. — compare Baudelaire, 'Les Phares' ("The Beacons"):

> Rembrandt, triste hôpital tout rempli de murmures,
> Et d'un grand crucifix décoré seulement,
> Où la prière en pleurs s'exhale des ordures,
> Et d'un rayon d'hiver traversé brusquement

---

[21] Letter to Armand Renaud, 27th June 1864 (*Correspondance*, 183-5). The Barbier and Millan *Poésies* (p. 203) reproduces a risqué triolet by Glatigny, 'L'Amoureuse de Mallarmé', which was published on the same page of the *Parnasse satyrique* as 'Une négresse…'

("Rembrandt, sad hospital all filled up with murmurs, / whose only decoration is a great crucifix, / where prayer breathes out in tears from filth, / abruptly crossed by a ray of winter sun").[22]

L. 25 — *je m'accroche à toutes les croisées*: "cross-panes" is clumsy for "croisées" ("casement windows"), but it seemed important to translate the "cross" element, here and in the sonnet "Ses purs ongles…" Roger Pearson[23] notes that the "croisées" are also the cross-rhymed stanzas ("rimes croisées") of the poem itself.

L. 26 — *D'où l'on tourne l'épaule à la vie* : Charles Gordon Millan[24] notes that it was only in 1893 that Mallarmé altered this phrase from its original form, "D'où l'on tourne le dos à la vie" ("from where one can turn one's back on life"), replacing a total rejection of life with a partial one. Jacques Villon, the eldest brother of Marcel Duchamp, named a 1939 etching[25] *D'où l'on tourne l'épaule à la vie,* in homage to the Mallarmé poem.

L. 32 — *où fleurit la Beauté*: "fleurit" can be either the present tense or past historic.

L. 37 — *ô Moi*: the poem as published in the *Parnasse* has "mon Dieu" here instead…

L. 39 — *mes deux ailes sans plume*: feathers always imply quill-pens in Mallarmé, so to be deprived of a "plume" becomes an image of artistic impotence or castration, here and in 'Don du poème'. Brigitte Léon-Dufour[26] suggests that the two "ailes" are actually the two 'L's of Mallarmé's surname, marking him out in advance for the wings of poesy.

---

[22] Noted by Takeo Kawase, 'A Crisis before "the Crisis": on Mallarmé's "Les Fenêtres"' in Robert Greer Cohn (ed.), *Mallarmé in the Twentieth Century*, 143-156, 146.

[23] *Unfolding Mallarmé*, 46.

[24] *Poésies* ed. Barbier and Millan, ix.

[25] In the collection of the Fine Arts Museum of San Francisco.

[26] 'Mallarmé et l'alphabet', *Cahiers de l'Association internationale des études françaises*, vol. 27 (1975), 321-343 (free online version at www.persee.fr).

The end of 'Les Fenêtres' is strongly echoed in Mallarmé's letter of 14th May 1867 to Henri Cazalis: "I have arrived, after a supreme synthesis, at this slow acquisition of strength — incapable, you will see, of relaxing. But how much worse it was several months ago, first in my terrible struggle with that old and spiteful plumage, now happily laid low, God. But as this struggle took place upon his bony wing, which, by a death-agony more vigorous than I would have suspected in him, had carried me into the Darkness, I fell, victorious, desperately and infinitely — until at last one day I saw myself again before my Venetian glass, and such as I was when I forgot myself several months before".[27]

Les Fleurs (page 30)

Written March 1864, and published in *Le Parnasse contemporain* of 12th May 1866. The poem as first published invoked God the Father rather than God the Mother, reading "Mon Dieu" for "Jadis" in line 3, "Notre Père" for "Notre dame" in the fifth quatrain, and "Ô Père" for "Ô Mère" in the sixth. The poem's vocabulary looks forward to 'Hérodiade' and to the giant flowers of 'Prose (pour des Esseintes)'.

L. 5-16 — this passage recalls the catalogue of flowers in Shelley's 'The Sensitive Plant',[28] which includes the lines

> And the hyacinth purple, and white, and blue,
> Which flung from its bells a sweet peal anew
> Of music so delicate, soft, and intense,
> It was felt like an odour within the sense;
>
> And the rose like a nymph to the bath addrest,
> Which unveiled the depth of her glowing breast,

---

[27] *Correspondance*, 342.
[28] A. Lytton Sells, 'Reflexions on Stéphane Mallarmé: Some Greek and English Reminiscences', *Modern Language Review*, 41 (1946), 362-381, 363. The reminiscence of Shelley was first noted by Albert Thibaudet.

Till, fold after fold, to the fainting air
The soul of her beauty and love lay bare;

And the wand-like lily, which lifted up,
As a Mænad, its moonlight-coloured cup,
Till the fiery star, which is its eye,
Gazed through clear dew on the tender sky

— Shelley's lines about the rose also seem to be echoed in the opening of Mallarmé's "Dame / sans trop d'ardeur…" and in the "pli selon pli" of 'Remémoration d'amis belges'. Henri Mondor[29] notes that Mallarmé was able to entertain friends at table by declaiming Shelley's poem.

L. 22 — *la future fiole*: compare the "fiole" in 'Éventail de Méry Laurent', and the sealed bottles of myrrh and rose-oil in 'Scène: Hérodiade' (line 29ff).

L. 23 — *la balsamique Mort*: both the future state of the flowers, embalmed and bottled as fragrance, and the toxic effect of these "fleurs du mal" on the tired poet. Compare the "poison tutélaire / Toujours à respirer si nous en périssons" at the end of 'Le Tombeau de Charles Baudelaire'.

L. 24 — *étiole*: one symptom of etiolation in plants is the growth of elongated stems. Compare 'Prose (pour des Esseintes)' lines 39-40: "de lis multiples la tige / Grandissait trop pour nos raisons".

Renouveau (page 34)

Written 1862, and published under the title 'Vere Novo' in *Le Parnasse contemporain* of 12th May 1866.

L. 5-6 — *mon crâne / Qu'un cercle de fer serre*: echoed in the opening quatrain of 'Prose (pour des Esseintes)', where memory is compared to a book bound in iron.

L. 12 — *ennui*: "boredom", but retaining some of the force of its presumed

---

[29] *Vie de Mallarmé*, 683.

etymon, the Latin "in odiō" (as in the phrase "mihī in odiō est" ["it is hateful to me"] — Littré/OED). The English cognate is "annoy".

Angoisse (page 36)

Written 1864 and published as 'À celle qui est tranquille' ("To one who is calm") in *Le Parnasse contemporain* of 12th May 1866. An earlier title was 'À une putain' ("To a whore").

L. 6 — *Planant sous les rideaux inconnus du remords*: compare Baudelaire, 'Les Deux Bonnes Sœurs':

> Tombeaux et lupanars montrent sous leurs charmilles
> Un lit que le remords n'a jamais fréquenté.

("Tombs and brothels display beneath their bowers / A bed remorse has never frequented").

L. 12 — *la dent d'aucun crime*: the tooth is that of remorse, etymologically a "biting again".[30]

"Las de l'amer repos où ma paresse offense…" (page 38)

Written 1864, and published under the title 'Epilogue' in *Le Parnasse contemporain* of 12th May 1866.

L. 5-6 — *creuser … le terrain… de ma cervelle*: "se creuser la tête" or "se creuser la cervelle" means "to rack one's brains".

L. 25 — *parmi le ciel de porcelaine nue*: Wayne K. Chapman[31] notes that this phrase can refer either back (to the lake) or forward (to the crescent moon). Chapman also spots the remarkable white-over-white non-image of the moon lost behind cloud, both represented by unpainted porcelain.

---

30 Robert Greer Cohn, *Toward the Poems of Mallarmé*, 21.
31 'Reading the Poem as Sentence and Music: Mallarmé's "Las de l'amer repos"', *Kentucky Romance Quarterly*, vol. 36 (1989), 15-26, 21.

L. 28 — *trois grands cils d'émeraude, roseaux*: compare the "cils" planted beside the eyes/lakes in the first version of 'Le Pitre châtié'.

Le Sonneur (page 42)

Published in the journal *L'Artiste*, 15th March 1862, and again in *Le Parnasse contemporain* of 12th May 1866.

L. 14 — *Ô Satan, j'ôterai la pierre et me pendrai*: echoed in the 'Ouverture ancienne d'Hérodiade', line 67f.: "Le croissant, oui le seul est au cadran de fer / De l'horloge, pour poids suspendant Lucifer".

Tristesse d'été (page 44)

Written 1862, and published in *Le Parnasse contemporain* of 30th June 1866. Originally grouped by Mallarmé with 'Renouveau' under the title 'Soleils Malsains' ("Unhealthy Suns"), later 'Soleils Mauvais' ("Bad Suns"). The joint title was dropped before either poem was published. Compare Baudelaire, 'La Géante' ("The Giantess"):

> Et parfois en été, quand les soleils malsains,
>
> Lasse, la font s'étendre à travers la campagne,
> Dormir nonchalamment à l'ombre de ses seins,
> Comme un hameau paisible au pied d'une montagne.

("And sometimes, in summer, when the unhealthy suns / make her stretch out wearily across the countryside, / to sleep indifferently in the shadow of her breasts / Like a peaceful village at the foot of a mountain").

There seems to be an unusual number of verbal parallels between this very Baudelairean early poem and 'Le Tombeau de Charles Baudelaire': "flamboiement" vs. "Tout le museau flambé"; the Egyptian "momie" vs. "Anubis"; "sans frissons" vs. "absente avec frissons". In Baudelaire's poem 'Le Squelette laboureur', "maint livre cadavéreux / Dort comme une antique momie" ("many a cadaverous book / sleeps like an antique mummy") in bookstalls on the dusty quays.

The earliest version of the poem reads:

> Le Soleil, sur la mousse où tu t'es endormie,
> A chauffé comme un bain tes cheveux ténébreux,
> Et, dans l'air sans oiseaux et sans brise ennemie,
> S'évapore ton fard en parfums dangereux.
>
> De ce blanc flamboiement l'immuable accalmie
> Me fait haïr la vie et notre amour fiévreux,
> Et tout mon être implore un sommeil de momie
> Morne comme le sable et les palmiers poudreux!
>
> Ta chevelure, est-elle une rivière tiède
> Où noyer sans frissons mon âme qui m'obsède
> Et jouir du Néant où l'on ne pense pas?
>
> Je veux boire le fard qui fond sous tes paupières
> Si ce poison promet au cœur que tu frappas
> L'insensibilité de l'azur et des pierres!

> ("The Sun upon the moss where you lie sleeping
> has warmed your dark hair like a bath
> and, into the air with no bird or hostile breeze,
> your make-up sublimates in unsafe perfumes.
>
> The changeless lull of this white blaze
> makes me hate life and our feverish love
> and all my being pleads for a mummy's sleep
> bleak as the sand and the dusty palm-trees!
>
> Is your hair a lukewarm river:

a place to drown, with no shiver, my soul that haunts me
and enjoy this Nothingness where one does not think?

I would drink the make-up melting under your eyelids
if this poison promises the heart you battered
the insensibility of the sky and stones!)

L'Azur (page 46)

Written 1864, and published in *Le Parnasse contemporain* of 12th May 1866.
Mallarmé gives a detailed account of the poem's composition in a letter to
Henri Cazalis of 7th[?] January 1864.[32]

L. 16 — *Les grands trous bleus que font méchamment les oiseaux*: one among
many images in Mallarmé of holes being pierced, often in the elements of air,
water or earth. Compare 'Le Pitre châtié' ("J'ai troué dans le mur de toile une
fenêtre", "dans l'onde j'innovais / Mille sépulcres"), "Las de l'amer repos…"
("creuser par veillée une fosse nouvelle / Dans le terrain avare et froid de
ma cervelle"), 'L'Après-midi d'un faune' ("Mon œil, trouant les joncs") and
"M'introduire dans ton histoire…" ("De voir en l'air que ce feu troue", which
also implicates the fourth element, fire). See also the note to line 8 of 'Aumône'.

L. 36 — Soon after the poem appeared in the *Parnasse*, Mallarmé (who was
an English teacher) arrived at school to find that one of the pupils (or perhaps
another teacher) had scrawled its astonishing last line on the blackboard.[33]
Mallarmé was quickly transferred to a different school.

Brise marine (page 50)

Written 1865, and published in *Le Parnasse contemporain* of 12th May 1866.

L. 2 — *Away! away!*: stolen for the translation from Keats's 'Ode to a
Nightingale': "Away! away! for I will fly to thee, / Not charioted by Bacchus

[32] *Correspondance*, 160-163.
[33] Henri Mondor, *Vie de Mallarmé*, 209.

and his pards, / But on the viewless wings of Poesy, / Though the dull brain perplexes and retards".

Soupir (page 52)

Written 1864, and published in *Le Parnasse contemporain* of 12th May 1866.

L. 8 — *lion-coloured*: stolen for the translation from Ezra Pound's "The Age Demanded" (from 'Mauberley 1920'): "The coral isle, the lion-coloured sand".

Aumône (page 54)

Published under the title 'À un pauvre' ("To a poor man"), in *Le Parnasse contemporain* of 12th May 1866. 'Aumône' seems to have been drafted around the same time as the related poem 'Haine du pauvre', dating from 1862 but not published until 1930, in *La Revue de France*:

Haine du pauvre

Ta guenille nocturne étalant par ses trous
Les rousseurs de tes poils et de ta peau, je l'aime
Vieux spectre, et c'est pourquoi je te jette vingt sous.

Ton front servile et bas n'a pas la fierté blême:
Tu comprends que le pauvre est le frère du chien
Et ne vas pas drapant ta lésine en poème.

Comme un chacal sortant de sa pierre, ô chrétien
Tu rampes à plat ventre après qui te bafoue.
Vieux, combien par grimace? et par larme, combien?

Mets à nu ta vieillesse et que la gueuse joue,
Lèche, et de mes vingt sous chatouille la vertu.
À bas!... — les deux genoux!... — la barbe dans la boue!

Que veut cette médaille idiote, ris-tu?

L'argent brille, le cuivre un jour se vert-de-grise,
Et je suis peu dévot et je suis fort têtu,

Choisis. — Jetée? alors, voici ma pièce prise.
Serre-la dans tes doigts et pense que tu l'as
Parce que j'en tiens trop, ou par simple méprise.

— C'est le prix, si tu n'as pas peur, d'un coutelas.

("Hatred of the poor"

Your night-time tatters flaunting through their holes
the redness of your hairs and skin, I love them
old spectre, and that is why I'm throwing you twenty sous.

Your low and servile brow lacks pallid pride:
you know the poor man is brother to the dog
and don't go dressing up your avarice in poetry.

Like a jackal leaving the shelter of a stone, o Christian
you crawl flat on your belly after those who mock you.
Old man, how much for a grimace? and per tear, how much?

Strip your old age naked and let the slattern play,
lick, and assay the virtue of my twenty sous.
Down!… — on both knees! … — with your beard in the mud!

What use is that stupid medal, do you laugh?
The silver shines, the copper will one day verdigris,
and I am scarce devout and very stubborn,

choose. — Thrown? so there, my coin is taken.
Grasp it between your fingers and think you have it

because I have too much, or simply by mistake.

— It is the price, if you have no fear, of a knife.")[34]

L. 8 — *berceur d'une bleue éclaircie*: the cloud-break, and the opium in line 10, also appear in the prose text 'Autrefois, en marge d'un Baudelaire' ("Long ago, in the margin of a copy of Baudelaire" from Mallarmé's 1897 prose book *Divagations*): "A landscape haunts with the intensity of opium; up above, and on the horizon, the livid cloud, with a blue gap of Prayer…"

L. 12 — *Et boire en la salive heureuse l'inertie*: clarified by an earlier draft, 'À un mendiant' ("To a beggar"):

> L'opium est à vendre en mainte pharmacie;
> Veux-tu mordre au rabais quelque pâle catin
> Et boire en sa salive un reste d'ambroisie?

("Opium is for sale in many a pharmacy: / do you want to bite some pallid, cut-rate whore / and drink an ambrosial rest in her saliva?")

Don du poème (page 58)

Written 1865, and published anonymously in *Paris Magazine. Grand Journal* of 23rd December 1866. The poem's title developed in successive drafts from 'Le Jour' through 'Le Poème nocturne', 'Dédicace du Poëme nocturne' and 'Don', to 'Don du poème'.

L. 1 — The kings of Idumea (the biblical Edom), according to the Kabbala, were

---

[34] Austin Gill (*The Early Mallarmé*, vol. 2, 218) sees the two poems as a diptych linked by rhyme ("coutelas / cajolas"). Note the metallurgical vocabulary in "Haine du pauvre": in line 10, a "gueuse", as well as being "a beggar-woman" or "female rascal" (personifying "ta viellesse"), can also be a "pig" (a mass of cast metal from a blast furnace). The phrase "chatouiller le remède" ("of coinage, to come very close to the maximum percentage of alloy that is legally permitted" — Littré), might also be behind "chatouille la vertu" in line 11.

sexless beings who reproduced without women.[35] The "child" is ambiguously 'Don du poème' itself, and the 'Scène: Hérodiade' which immediately follows it in the 1899 *Poésies*, and for which 'Don du poème' serves as a dedication (the biblical Herodias, mother of Salome, was the grand-daughter of Herod's sister Salome I, and of Costabarus, governor of Idumea).

L. 5-6 — *lampe ... Palmes*: the almost-anagrams suggest an image of the lamp reflected in the window (or the line-break). Henri Mondor and G. Jean-Aubry[36] quote a couplet from Boileau, *Satire IX*, which has idumean palms and an almost-rhyme on *Mallarmé*:

> Et, passant du Jourdain les ondes alarmées,
> Cueillir, mal à propos, les palmes idumées?

("And, crossing the troubled waves of the Jordan, / To gather, inappositely, idumean palms?") Boileau's lines are part of a catalogue of poetic clichés,[37] and an echo of them would reinforce the impression that the child born of night in 'Don du poème' is an incomplete, antiquated, even horrible thing.

L. 12 — *presseras-tu le sein*: Jeffrey Mehlman[38] notes the formal coincidence of French "sein" ("breast") and German "Sein" ("Being"); Mallarmé's wife, Maria Gerhard, was German, and their daughter Geneviève was raised bilingual.[39]

---

[35] See Denis Saurat, 'La nuit d'Idumée: Mallarmé et la Cabale', in Saurat, *Perspectives*, 113-116, 114.

[36] *OC*, 1439, which also traces the Idumean palms back to Virgil, *Georgics*, III, 12. Austin Gill, *The Early Mallarmé*, vol. 1, 72 n. 50 notes that Mallarmé would have read Boileau's *Satires* as a pupil at the Lycée in Sens.

[37] See Boileau, *Œuvres complètes*, 923, and Barbara Johnson, 'Les Fleurs du Mal Armé: Some Reflections on Intertextuality', in *A World of Difference*, 116-133, 130 and 219 n.8.

[38] Denis Hollier and Jeffrey Mehlman (eds.), *Literary Debate: texts and contexts*, 175.

[39] Marie-Thérèse Stanislas, *Geneviève Mallarmé-Bonniot*, 9.

Ouverture ancienne d'Hérodiade (page 60)

Written 1866. Published posthumously in *La Nouvelle Revue française* of 1st November 1926, in a version edited from the unfinalised draft by Mallarmé's son-in-law Edmond Bonniot. Gardner Davies (ed.), *Les Noces d'Hérodiade. Mystère* gives a variorum text of all drafts and notes relating to the 'Hérodiade' project, which occupied Mallarmé at intervals from 1864 until his death.[40]

In neither of the biblical accounts of the story of Salome and John the Baptist (Mark 6:17-29 and Matt. 14:2-11) is the girl given a name (the name "Salome" comes from Josephus's *Jewish Antiquities*). Mallarmé follows an alternative tradition in which the girl is given the same name as her mother, Herodias. This serves to emphasise his Hérodiade's flight from sex: "Hérodiade, daughter of Hérodiade" suggests that she arose from a process more like duplication or cloning than sexual reproduction. In a letter to Eugène Lefébure of 18th February 1965, Mallarmé wrote: "The most beautiful page of my work will be the one which contains only that divine name Hérodiade. What little inspiration I have had, I owe to this name, and I believe that if my heroine had been called Salome, I would have invented that sombre word, red as an open pomegranate".[41]

Mallarmé's letter of 28th April 1866 to Henri Cazalis compares the then-new 'Ouverture' favourably to the 'Scène' which was the only fragment of 'Hérodiade' to be published during Mallarmé's lifetime: "I have spent [three months] working relentlessly on 'Hérodiade', as my lamp knows! I have written the musical overture, still almost completely in first draft, but I can say without presumption that it will have an unheard-of effect, and that the dramatic scene you already know, next to these verses, is but a vulgar *Image d'Épinal* [a kind of popular coloured print] compared to a canvas by Leonardo

---

[40] The drafts and fragments have been substantially re-edited by Bertrand Marchal for tome 1 of his edition of Mallarmé's *Œuvres complètes*. According to this edition (p. 1221) the following lines of the 'Ouverture' were scored-out in pencil in the latest surviving draft: lines 17-19, line 58 (and the first word of line 59), and lines 90-97.
[41] *Correspondance*, 226.

da Vinci".[42]

The English "pen", meaning "female swan" might underwrite some of the feather imagery in the poem.

L. 26 — *un passé de ramages*: "passé" can mean "past" as well as a kind of embroidery; "ramage" can mean "bird-song" as well as a leaf- or flower pattern on cloth.

L. 52-53 — *Elle, encore, l'antienne aux versets demandeurs, / À l'heure d'agonie et de luttes funèbres!*: an anticipation of the 'Cantique' sung by Saint John at the moment of his death.[43]

L. 58 — *Elle a chanté*: "Elle" is both Hérodiade and the feminine noun "voix" from the preceding stanza.

L. 59 — *le lit aux pages de vélin*: the bed is a book because "lit" is also a verb form meaning "he/she/it reads".[44] A bed with pages could also be a "divan", meaning "a collection in Arabic or Persian of poems by one poet". One section of *Divagations* is entitled 'Volumes sur le divan'.

L. 67ff. — *Le croissant [...] Toujours blesse*: the crescent that always wounds is also the scythe that beheads John the Baptist in the 'Cantique de saint Jean'. The whole passage might be read as evoking the "lunar wound" of menstruation: time passes, and Hérodiade (whose father is still paying her wet-nurse) is herself the clepsydra, weeping a dark drop, and the pomegranate cut by evening. A number of fragments of *Les Noces d'Hérodiade* suggest images of menstruation, at least as much as they suggest hymeneal blood, or the blood of the Baptist: "chair, encor san- / glottante d'avoir été / niée" ("flesh, still bleed- / ing from having been / denied"); "— idée / saigne — sang sur ses cuisses /

---

[42] *Correspondance*, 297.

[43] Noted by Gardner Davies, 'Mallarmé's "Le Cantique de Saint Jean"', *Essays in French Literature,* vol. 1 (1964), 7-29, 8.

[44] Noted by Jacques Derrida, 'The Double Session', in *Dissemination* (tr. Barbara Johnson), 224, with reference to Mallarmé's short prose text 'Mimique'.

220

pourpre des cuisses / et leur royauté" ("— idea / bleeds — blood on her thighs / purple of the thighs / and their royalty").[45]

L. 68 — *pour poids suspendant Lucifer*: Lucifer is the planet Venus seen as the morning star, bringer of light. "L'horloge" is the name of a constellation: Horologium (The Clock).

Scène: Hérodiade (page 68)

Published under the title 'Fragment d'une étude scénique ancienne d'un poëme de Hérodiade' in the second series of *Le Parnasse contemporain* (dated 1869 but not distributed until November 1871 because of the Franco-Prussian War).

L. 8 — *Si la beauté n'était la mort*: beauty and death are also linked in the final stanza of 'Prose (pour des Esseintes)', though less inexorably than in Hérodiade's equation.

L. 14 — *les mains sauves*: lions were reputed never to harm virgins.[46] The passage is oddly reminiscent of the end of William Blake's poem 'Little Girl Lost', where the friendly lioness undresses the sleeping Lyca.

L. 23 — *mes pieds qui calmeraient la mer*: almost the same phrase appears in a poem written in 1862, 'L'Enfant prodigue' ("The Prodigal son"):

> Tes genoux qu'ont durcis les oraisons rêveuses,
> Je les baise, et tes pieds qui calmeraient la mer;
> Je veux plonger ma tête en tes cuisses nerveuses
> Et pleurer mon erreur sous ton cilice amer

("Your knees, calloused by dreamlike prayers, / I kiss them, and your feet that would becalm the sea; / I want to plunge my head between your firm thighs / and weep my error beneath your bitter hair-shirt").

L. 29 — *la myrrhe gaie*: given the incestuous overtones of the biblical story of

---

[45] Marchal (ed.) *OC*, tome 1, 1087 and 1094.
[46] F.C. St. Aubyn, *Stéphane Mallarmé*, 50.

Salome/Hérodias and Herod, there might be an echo here of Ovid's legend (*Metamorphoses*, Book X) of Myrrha, the daughter of Cinyras, king of Cyprus, who seduced her father with the help of her aged nurse.

L. 30 — *aux vieillesses de roses*: compare the forsaken "enfance / Adorable des bois de roses" in "Las de l'amer repos…"

L. 44ff. — *Ô miroir*: compare this passage with Mallarmé's prose poem 'Frisson d'hiver' ("Winter shiver"): "And your Venetian glass, deep as a cold spring, set in a shoreline of wyverns[47] losing their gilding, who has been mirrored there? Ah! I am sure that more than one woman has bathed the sin of her beauty in this water; and perhaps, if I looked for a long time, I might see a naked phantom."

L. 52-53 — *Un astre, en vérité / Mais cette tresse tombe*: Hérodiade is being compared to a comet, etymologically "un astre chevelu" or "long-haired star" (Littré).

L. 110 — *ta sœur solitaire, ô ma sœur éternelle*: either the moon,[48] or Hérodiade's own reflection in the mirror.[49]

L. 112 — *Rare limpidité d'un cœur qui le songea*: compare the "Chinois au cœur limpide et fin" of "Las de l'amer repos…" Hérodiade's soliloquy gives some idea of what it might be like actually to live in the abstracted world the poet flees to in the earlier poem.

L. 134 — *Se séparer enfin ses froides pierreries*: grammatically, the "pierreries" can't separate: according to Littré, the word is never used in the singular. The illicit singular "pierrerie" in "Au seul souci de voyager…" might be an ironic fulfilment of Hérodiade's wish.

---

[47] The wyvern (French "guivre") might be there because of the mythical beast's reputed fear of naked human beings (see Karl Shuker, *Dragons: a Natural History*, 17).
[48] F.C. St. Aubyn, *Stéphane Mallarmé*, 56.
[49] A.R. Chisholm, *Towards Hérodiade*, 159.

Cantique de saint Jean (page 86)

Published posthumously in the 1913 *Poésies*.[50]

L. 1 — *sa halte*: the feast of John the Baptist, 24th June, follows the summer solstice (20th-23rd June), the time when the sun reaches its highest point north of the celestial equator and starts to descend again. "Solstice" is from Latin "sol" ("sun") and "sistere" ("to stand still"). Mallarmé's phrase has also been interpreted as a reference to the moment when the sun appears to stand still on the horizon just before setting.[51]

L. 3-4 — *redescend / Incandescent*: Edward J.H. Greene[52] notes the echo of this rhyme in T.S. Eliot's 'Little Gidding', part IV:

> The dove descending breaks the air
> With flame of incandescent terror

— Eliot's lines also recall the piercing of air by fire in "M'introduire dans ton histoire...", and of air by birds in 'L'Azur'.

L. 6 — *S'éployer*: L.J. Austin[53] describes this as a verb recreated by Mallarmé from the adjective "éployé", used in heraldry to designate an eagle with outspread wings.

L. 23 — *Que vous le surpassiez*: Gardner Davies[54] notes that the masculine pronoun "le" must refer back to "Son pur regard" rather than to the more

---

[50] Page scans of the 1913 edition can be viewed online at the University of Michigan Digital General Collection, http://quod.lib.umich.edu

[51] See Gardner Davies, 'Mallarmé's "Le Cantique de Saint Jean"', *Essays in French Literature*, vol. 1 (1964), 7-29, 9. In Davies' own interpretation of the first stanza, the sun is seen by its reflection in the executioner's blade, momentarily immobilised before the blade falls.

[52] *T.S. Eliot et La France*, 138.

[53] *Essais sur Mallarmé*, 155.

[54] Davies, *art. cit.*, 21.

proximate, but feminine, "la froidure / Éternelle".

L'Après-midi d'vn favne (page 90)

Published 1876 in a deluxe edition with illustrations by Édouard Manet.

Title and subtitles — the archaising "v" for "u" is in all early editions.

L. 7 — *la faute idéale de roses*: as well as "ideal error", "la faute idéale" could be the "ideal sin" or "ideal lack" of roses.

L. 34 — *Trop d'hymen*: both too much hymen, and too much marriage.[55] A nymph is etymologically a "bride"; "les nymphes", in French, are the labia minora.[56]

L. 34 — *qui cherche le la*: the reference is to tuning a musical instrument,[57] though the whole poem could be considered a quest for "the feminine definite article".[58]

L. 69 — *ce mal d'être deux*: this contrasts with the positive insistence on duality in 'Prose (pour des Esseintes)' line 10, "Nous fûmes deux, je le maintiens".

L. 70 — *Des dormeuses parmi leurs seuls bras hasardeux*: Robert Greer Cohn[59] relates this passage to one in Keats's 'Ode to Psyche':

> I wander'd in a forest thoughtlessly,
>   And, on the sudden, fainting with surprise,
> Saw two fair creatures, couched side by side
>   In deepest grass, beneath the whisp'ring roof
>   Of leaves and trembled blossoms [...]

[55] The Mallarméan 'hymen' is a crux of Jacques Derrida's essay "The Double Session" (in *Dissemination*, tr. Barbara Johnson). Robert Greer Cohn (*Mallarmé's Divagations: A Guide and Commentary*, 167-172) argues that it needn't have been so.

[56] Roger Pearson, *Unfolding Mallarmé*, 118.

[57] L.J Austin, *Essais sur Mallarmé*, 187.

[58] See Jacques Derrida, 'Mallarmé', in *Acts of Literature*, 119.

[59] 'Keats and Mallarmé', *Comparative Literature Studies*, vol. 7 (1970), 195-203, 202.

They lay calm-breathing on the bedded grass;
 Their arms embraced, and their pinions too;
 Their lips touch'd not, but had not bade adieu
As if disjoined by soft-handed slumber,
And ready still past kisses to outnumber...

L. 90 — *défaits par de vagues trépas*: the faun is momentarily distracted by his own orgasm, "la petite mort".[60]

L. 95-96 — *pourpre et déjà mûre, / Chaque grenade éclate et d'abeilles murmure*: a pointed contrast with the pomegranates that only open when cut by spiteful evening in the 'Ouverture ancienne d'Hérodiade' (line 66).

L. 101 — *Etna! c'est parmi toi visité de Vénus*: a similar vision of Venus as the evening star (which the drunken faun, here, confuses with the goddess) occurs in 'Scène: Hérodiade', line 124f.: "les regards haïs / De Vénus qui, le soir, brûle dans le feuillage". The name "Vénus" appears exactly ten lines before the end of each poem.

L. 109 — *l'astre efficace des vins*: literally, "the star that causes wine".

Marcel Duchamp's 1924 photocollage *Monte Carlo Bond*[61] (signed jointly with Rrose Sélavy) superimposes a cropped photograph of Duchamp's head, smothered in foam and with his hair teased up into two horns, on an image of a roulette wheel — a triply-Mallarméan image of *écume*, *faune* and *hasard*. One might also see an image of the beheaded John the Baptist in this head presented on the platter of a roulette wheel, and link the 'Bond' in "Monte Carlo Bond" with the "bond hagard" (a wild, or haggard, bounce or leap) of the head in the 'Cantique de saint Jean'.[62]

---

[60] F.C. St. Aubyn, *Stéphane Mallarmé*, 67.
[61] Reproduced in Gavin Parkinson, *The Duchamp Book*, 147. Parkinson (p.56) notes that Duchamp greatly admired Mallarmé, and had been reading him since at least 1911.
[62] Sheldon Nodelman ('Duchampiana: The Decollation of Saint Marcel', *Art in America*, vol. 94 no. 9 (2006), 107-119) reads an echo of Duchamp's reading of Mallarmé into a

"La chevelure vol d'une flamme à l'extrême…" (page 100)

Published in the journal *L'Art et la mode* of 12th August 1887, as part of the prose poem 'La Déclaration foraine' (later collected in *Divagations*).

L. 1 — *vol*: primarily "flight", but also the Promethean "theft" of a flame.

L. 1-2 — *l'extrême / Occident*: a play on "l'Extrême-Orient" ("The Far East").

L. 2 — *éployer*: for this verb, see the notes to 'Cantique de saint Jean'. The verb's proximity to "vol", "flamme" and "se pose" suggests a burning bird, recalling the "Phénix" of the sonnet "Ses purs ongles…" The poem as originally published in 'La Déclaration foraine' has "déployer" here instead.

L. 4 — *couronné*: Michael Temple[63] notes that Mallarmé's first name, Stéphane, means "crown" in Greek.

L. 5 — *Mais sans or soupirer que cette vive nue*: this remarkably polyvalent line could also be translated "but without sighing for any gold other than this live cloud" or "but without sighing for gold, let this live cloud"[64] (both alternatives would require "continue" in line 7 to be read as indicative rather than subjunctive). The verb forms "se pose", "diffame" and "écorche" are similarly ambiguous in mood: it's impossible to tell whether the poem is describing potential, or only actual, events.

L. 5 — *vive nue*: this phrase has an exact antonym in the "défunte nue" of "Ses purs ongles…"[65]

1937 staged photograph (possibly taken by Man Ray) of Mary Reynolds posing with Duchamp's disembodied head.

[63] *The Name of the Poet: Onomastics and Anonymity in the Works of Stéphane Mallarmé*, 91.

[64] See Edward J. Ahearn, "'Simplifier avec gloire la femme": Syntax, Synecdoche, Subversion in a Mallarmé Sonnet', *The French Review*, vol. 58 no. 3 (1985), 349-359. "Or" could also be read as the conjunction meaning "now", "although", "yet", "but"; "continue" as the adjective meaning "continuous"; and "tendre" as the adjective meaning "tender". Barbara Johnson (*The Critical Difference: Essays in the Contemporary Rhetoric of Reading*, 61f) gives a useful diagram, in exploded view, of the poem's possibilities.

[65] *Poésies* ed. Marchal,.219.

L. 12 — *chef*: an archaic masculine word for "head". The first example phrase given in the definition of "chef" in Littré is "Le chef de saint Jean-Baptiste"…

L. 12 — *fulgurante*: the feminine adjective qualifies "la femme" rather than one of the two masculine nouns on either side of it. For Edward J. Ahearn,[66] the adjective summons up the ghost of the regular (and feminine) French word for head, "la tête".

L. 12 — *l'exploit*: etymologically an unfolding;[67] the line fulfils the desire for unfolding (or spreading of wings) expressed in line 2.

L. 13 — *semer de rubis*: compare Claude de Malleville's 17th century sonnet 'La Belle matineuse': "L'Aurore déployoit l'or de sa tresse blonde / Et semoit de rubis le chemin du Soleil" ("The Dawn was spreading the gold of her blond tresses / and strewing the Sun's path with rubies"). See also Baudelaire's poem 'La Chevelure': "Longtemps! toujours! ma main dans ta crinière lourde / Sèmera le rubis, la perle et le saphir" ("For a long time! always! my hand in your heavy mane / will scatter ruby, pearl and sapphire").

L. 13 — *écorche*: often translated as the anglicism "scorch", which both fits the flame imagery and rhymes with "torch".

Sainte (page 102)

Original title 'Sainte Cécile jouant sur l'aile d'un chérubin' ("Saint Cecilia playing on the wing of a cherub"). Written in 1865 for the saint's day of Cécile Brunet, the godmother of Mallarmé's daughter Geneviève and wife of the poet and master-glassmaker Jean Brunet.[68] Published in Verlaine's essay on Mallarmé in the journal *Lutèce*, 24-30th November 1883.

The poem might contain an echo of Poe's 'Israfel', the angel "Whose heart-strings are a lute". See also Mallarmé's prose poem 'Le Démon de l'analogie'

---

[66] Ahearn, *art. cit.*, 356.
[67] A.R. Chisholm, *Mallarmé's grand œuvre*, 22.
[68] *OC,* 1468.

("The Demon of analogy"), which opens with "the clear sensation of a wing gliding over the strings of an instrument".[69]

Toast funèbre (page 104)

Published 1873 in the commemorative, multi-authored volume *Le Tombeau de Théophile Gautier.*[70]

L. 11 — *ce beau monument*: the commemorative volume, as much as the tomb. In a passage from 'Le livre, instrument spirituel' ("The book, spiritual instrument", from *Divagations*), Mallarmé refers to the pages of a book, settled into a block, as "offering a minuscule tomb, certainly, for the soul".

L. 18-19 — *Nous sommes / La triste opacité de nos spectres futurs*: rather than being a ghost of its former self, the crowd is a self of its future ghost...

L. 22 — *sourd même à mon vers sacré qui ne l'alarme*: the passer(-by) fails to be "alarmé" by Mallarmé.

L. 23 — *Quelqu'un de ces passants*: a "passant" is both a passer-by and someone in the process of dying, of "passing on".[71]

L. 27 — *l'irascible vent des mots qu'il n'a pas dits*: the predicament of the passer(-by), abolished in the gulf of his own failure either to have perceived the Earth or to have said anything about it, is very similar to that of the swan in "Le vierge, le vivace et le bel aujourd'hui…", doomed for never having sung a place to live.

L. 28 — *cet Homme aboli de jadis*: Robert Greer Cohn[72] notes that "jadis" implies that this Man was "abolished" long before he actually died.

L. 32 — *Le Maître, par un œil profond*: in a letter to François Coppée[73] dating

---

[69] Noted by Bradford Cook, *Mallarmé: Selected Prose Poems, Essays and Letters*, 109.

[70] Paris: Lemerre 1873. The book can be downloaded as a pdf file from http://gallica.bnf.fr/

[71] Robert Greer Cohn, *Toward the Poems of Mallarmé*, 101.

[72] *Toward the Poems of Mallarmé*, 103.

[73] Quoted *OC*, 1470.

from early 1873, Mallarmé writes: "I will sing, in couplets, one of Gautier's glorious qualities: the mysterious gift of seeing with the eyes (delete mysterious). I will sing the seer, who, placed in this world, looked at it, which is not done."

L. 47 — *Isole parmi l'heure et le rayon du jour*: this line is very reminiscent of the midday island of 'Prose (pour des Esseintes)': 'isoler' is derived from Latin 'insulatus' ('separated like an island' — Littré). The two poems (placed next to one another near the centre of the *Poésies* and both 56 lines long) are closely associated, but Mallarmé seems to be making a distinction between Gautier's use of language and his own.[74] In 'Toast funèbre', Gautier *names* the rose and lily, and the poet's 'regard diaphane' isolates, irradiates and perpetuates his own verbal flowers. In 'Prose (pour des Esseintes)', the vision of the flowers in hyperbolic growth is something that is claimed (though in words) to take place in the absence of language ("Sans que nous en devisions"), and that shocks the observer into silence. See the notes to 'Prose (pour des Esseintes)' for more on Mallarmé and naming.

Prose (pour des Esseintes) (page 110)

Published January 1885 in *La Revue indépendante*, and dedicated to Duc Jean Floressas des Esseintes, the aesthete hero of J.-K. Huysmans' novel *À Rebours* ("Against the Grain", 1884). Mallarmé was one of des Esseintes' favourite authors: chapter 14 of the novel quotes from 'Scène: Hérodiade' and 'L'Après-midi d'un faune', and praises Mallarmé's prose poems in particular. The jury seems still to be out on whether Mallarmé wrote the poem in response to Huysmans' novel, or simply added the dedication, and possibly the last two stanzas, to a poem written much earlier, perhaps in the 1870s.[75]

Title — *Prose*: both a reference to the *prosa*, a kind of rhymed Latin hymn sung

---

[74] See Leo Bersani, *The Death of Stéphane Mallarmé*, 28ff.
[75] See Graham Robb, *Unlocking Mallarmé*, Appendix II, 222 for a discussion of the poem's date. Marshall C. Olds, *Desire Seeking Expression: Mallarmé's "Prose pour des Esseintes"* includes a useful critical bibliography.

in some types of Catholic mass (so called because of its accentual metre; *versus* was reserved for quantitative verse)[76] and a joke that this exceptionally complex poem might seem like plain prose to des Esseintes. In Mallarmé's prose poem 'Plainte d'automne' (referred to in *À Rebours* and concerned, like 'Prose (pour des Esseintes)', with the memory of a sister), the "infantile Latin of the first Christian prosae" is contrasted with that "dying poetry of the final moments of Rome" so dear to the narrator of 'Plainte d'automne' (and to des Esseintes).

L. 1 — *Hyperbole*: either "hyperbole" (a figure of speech using exaggeration for emphasis) or "hyperbola" (in geometry, a conic section consisting of two diverging, discontinuous curve segments, extending to infinity), both from the Greek for "a throwing beyond, or excess". The similar ambiguity of the French word "parabole" (either a parable or a parabola — another type of conic section), might be relevant: 'Prose', the most narrative-like of Mallarmé's *Poésies*, would then be, if not a parable, then something like a "hyper-parable". L.J. Austin[77] cites Baudelaire's essay on the poet Théodore de Banville: "First of all, note that hyperbole and apostrophe are those forms of language which are not only most agreeable to [de Banville], but also most necessary..." — Mallarmé's homage in the first word of 'Prose' would thus consist in *apostrophising hyperbole*. The geometrical sense of "hyperbole"[78] is reflected in the poem's insistence on doubleness, and the flower-stalks that grow beyond all reason — and given that the poem seems to take place around noon, it's also worth noting that a hyperbola is the shape traced out by the shadow of the tip of a sundial's gnomon, with the turning-point corresponding to local noon. The collection of a year's-worth of these hyperbolas is called a "pelekinon", from the Greek for a kind of double-headed axe: this echo of an echo might hold an echo of the beheading of John the Baptist (and of at least three of the saints called Anastasius, for whom see line 51).

---

[76] OED, *Prose*, 2.

[77] *Poetic principles and practice*, 84.

[78] For more on the hyperbola, see Roger Pearson, *Unfolding Mallarmé*, 219.

L. 3 — *grimoire*: a gramarye, "a book of occult learning or magic". The French word (also used in 'Scène: Hérodiade' and the Wagner 'Hommage') can also mean "obscure writing" or "gibberish".

L. 5 — *Car j'installe, par la science*: E. Noulet notes the very strong insistence on conscious artistry here, refuting in advance any attempt at a psychoanalytic interpretation of the work.[79]

L. 9 — *Nous promenions notre visage*: a play on the expression "promener ses regards sur quelque chose" ("to cast one's eye over something").

L. 12 — *O sœur*: the "sœur" has been identified with Mallarmé's own sister Maria (who died at the age of thirteen), with the poet's soul or anima, with the Muse and with more or less all of the feminine nouns in the first two stanzas of the poem. E. Noulet[80] makes a good case for the "sœur sensée et tendre" being a personification of "ma patience", though Charles Chadwick's identification of the sister with "Hyperbole"[81] (the first entity in the poem to be addressed as "tu") is also appealing. Among other merits, it makes for a neat reversal of roles between the beginning and end of the poem: in the first stanza, the speaker wants "Hyperbole" to "raise itself (or herself)" from his memory. By stanza thirteen, it's the "sœur" who is learned enough to issue the injunction "raise yourself!" (and in Greek, too). It might be worth remembering that the Muses are the daughters of memory ("de ma mémoire"),[82] and that "Hyperbole" is a quite plausible name for a supernumerary Muse.

L. 12 — *y comparant les tiens*: the only other instance of "comparer" in the *Poésies (sensu lato)* is in "Une negresse…", where the protagonist compares her two nipples on (or to) her belly: the sister's charms might not, then, be exclusively spiritual.

---

[79] *Vingt poèmes de Stéphane Mallarmé*, 116 and 123.
[80] *Vingt poèmes*, 108.
[81] Quoted in Noulet, *Vingt poèmes*, 107.
[82] Noted by Roger Pearson, *Unfolding Mallarmé*, 222 n. 41.

L. 15 — *ce midi*: Roger Pearson[83] notes the French slang "marquer midi" ("to have an erection") in relation both to this poem and 'L'Après-midi d'un faune'.[84]

L. 16 — *approfondit*: the verb "approfondir" can either mean "to make something deeper" or "to go more deeply into something". "Approfondit" can be either the present tense or the past historic.

L. 17 — The irises/*iridées* are principally flowers, but the visual intensity of the poem's *regards* makes the ocular sense relevant too: these are flowers that return the gaze. Section II of Ezra Pound's 'Mauberley (1920)' plays on the same ambiguity:

> He had passed, inconscient, full gaze,
> The wide-banded irides
> And botticellian sprays implied
> In their diastasis;

— "sprays" implies flowers (as well as the birth of Venus from sea-spray), "diastasis" means "a colobomatous defect of the peripheral part of the iris, leaving the pupillary border intact".[85] Given the context, Pound's rather odd use of "inconscient" might be an echo of the "Inconscience" in quatrain 4 of 'Prose'.

The Greek messenger-goddess Iris seems also to be a presence in the poem. Hesiod (*Theogony*, line 780ff.) describes how, whenever strife and quarrelling break out among the gods of Olympus, Zeus sends Iris to draw a pitcher of water from the river Styx. Any god who perjures him- or herself while under an oath sworn upon this water must lie for a year deprived of spirit, breath and voice, and then endure nine years of exile. The poem's speaker and his sister

---

[83] *Unfolding Mallarmé*, 171 n.12.
[84] For a link between this and the suggested sundial imagery, see Hubert's method of telling the time in Vivian Stanshall, *Sir Henry at Rawlinson End* (Virgin Chattering Classics CD, 1995).
[85] Definition of *iridodiastasis* from *Butterworth's Medical Dictionary*.

have their hour of silence, but they insist (to the Spirit of litigation, possibly Iris herself) that this is not because the island of flowers does not exist (which is a lie promulgated by the monotonous play of the riverbank, and by the false witness borne by the sky and map). Iris's pitcher also links this poem to the sonnet "Ses purs ongles…", where "le Maître est allé puiser des pleurs au Styx".[86] Penultimately, Iris was also the goddess who led young girls into the afterlife.[87]

L. 19 — *ne porte pas de nom*: Mallarmé famously wrote "To *name* an object is to remove three-quarters of the pleasure ('jouissance') of the poem, which is made to be discovered little by little: to *suggest* it, that is the dream."[88] The era of authority, in 'Prose', is "troubled" ("se troubler", like "jouissance", can have a sexual connotation) by the possibility that the landscape might bear no name. A "name", in the final stanza, is the kind of thing a gravestone might bear, and the poem's various strategies for avoiding naming are really strategies for evading death. Silence, whether owed to astonishment or infancy ("enfant" is from Latin "infans", meaning "speechless") works, up to a point, but children grow up to abdicate their ecstasy. The distinction between "mot" and "nom" in the last two stanzas of the poem seems crucial. "Anastase" and "Pulchérie" are proper names, and when used as such they retain only a tenuous ghost of meaning from the common nouns from which they were derived: a woman named Pulchérie need not be beautiful. By calling "Anastase" a "word", Mallarmé resurrects the dead meaning locked in a name derived from a word meaning "resurrect" — and it is by means of such transgressions, and the complexities and undecidabilities in which the poem abounds, that 'Prose (pour des Esseintes)' maintains its own, perhaps not immortal, but perpetually unnameable, indefinable[89] life.

L. 29 — *Gloire*: as well as glory, the word implies the iridescence of the flowers

---

[86] Noted by Roger Pearson, *Unfolding Mallarmé*, 164 n. 12.
[87] Debra N. Mancoff, *Flora Symbolica: Flowers in Pre-Raphaelite Art*, 16.
[88] *OC*, 869.
[89] The first word of the earliest surviving draft of the poem is "Indéfinissable".

within their lucid contour (a "glory" or small rainbow-coloured halo,[90] once again recalling the goddess Iris, a personification of the rainbow).

L. 41-48 — to be understood as "and not, as the shoreline weeps, … that this country did not exist" with a long parenthesis intervening. Much depends upon whether "attestés" is taken to mean "attested" or "called upon to bear witness". The latter sense has the advantage of providing an alternate route out of the long syntax ("called upon to bear witness … that this country did not exist"),[91] and of echoing the verb "citer" in line 19, which can also mean "to summon a witness". D.J. Mossop[92] notes that astronomy and geography ("tout le ciel et la carte") were constantly being invoked, in Mallarmé's day as in ours, to testify to the non-existence of Paradise.

L. 51 — *Anastase*: a French spelling of the proper name "Anastasius", from the Greek for "a rising up, erection or resurrection" — a meaning which parallels that of "Hyperbole!" in line 1, "Te lever" in line 3, and "Surgir" in line 32. The name of two Byzantine emperors, four popes and something like twenty saints (one of them a tenth-century archbishop of Sens, the town where Mallarmé went to secondary school).[93] The nineteenth-century technology of "anastatic printing",[94] whereby handwritten documents or drawings could be transferred directly to a zinc plate for printing, might also be relevant here: that would be one way to create "eternal parchments". Edgar Allan Poe published an essay entitled 'Anastatic Printing' in 1845 (first collected in the 1874-5 edition of Poe's *Works* edited by John H. Ingram).[95] Mallarmé's own 1887 *Poésies* was

---

[90] See Marshall C. Olds, *Desire Seeking Expression*, 37.

[91] See L. J. Austin, *Essais sur Mallarmé*, 131 n.106.

[92] 'Mallarmé's Prose Pour des Esseintes', *French Studies,* vol. 18 (1964), 123-135, 134.

[93] www.catholic.org, article on St. Anastasius XVIII. See also M. l'Abbé Brullée, 'Notice sur saint Anastase, 60me archevêque de Sens', in *Bulletin de la Société archéologique de Sens* (1854), 57-62 (this volume can be read online at http://gallica.bnf.fr/).

[94] Noted by Heath Lees, *Mallarmé and Wagner*, 180.

[95] Published in Edinburgh by Adam and Charles Black. The 'Scolies' to Mallarmé's Poe translations (*OC,* 227 and 246) refer to Ingram's "English" editions of Poe, so

published as a facsimile of his own handwriting (though by photolithography, not anastatic printing).

L. 54: *Sous aucun climat*: compare Baudelaire's poem 'Danse macabre': "En tout climat, sous tout soleil, la Mort t'admire / En tes contorsions, risible Humanité" ("In every climate, under every sun, Death admires you / in your contortions, laughable Humanity"). "Aucun climat" can mean "any climate" or "no climate"; for Littré (*Aucun*, remarque 7), the word is eymologically and historically affirmative, the negative sense developing from its frequent collocation with the particle "ne". Here, the phrase implies a falling away from the localised "midi" of the island into the big world of generation(s) and death, located everywhere and nowhere.

L. 55 — *Pulchérie*: a French spelling of the proper name "Pulcheria", from the Latin for "beauty". The name of an empress of the Eastern Roman Empire (*fl.* 399-453), later venerated as a saint. Pulcheria is a patron saint of orphans, and her emblem is a lily. Graham Robb[96] notes the way in which "sépulcre ne rie" and "Pulchérie" are forced into looking like a better rhyme, a more perfect equation of beauty and death, than they actually are.

L. 56 — *glaïeul*: also an alternative French name for the yellow flag *Iris pseudacorus*. Littré gives "petit glaive" ("little sword") as the etymology of "glaïeul", which would make the line pleasingly oxymoronic: "hidden by the too-large small sword". Graham Robb[97] notes that "cacher sous des fleurs" means "to conceal something dangerous under an attractive surface": here it functions as a last humorous undermining of the finality of death, as if the destructive power of naming could be negated simply by hiding the name. Shakespeare's 65th Sonnet, in which the plea held by beauty against the rage of sad mortality has an action no stronger than a flower, makes a parallel case.

Mallarmé would have known at least one edition of Poe's works which included 'Anastatic Printing'.

[96] *Unlocking Mallarmé*, 176.

[97] *Unlocking Mallarmé*, 169.

Éventail de Madame Mallarmé (page 116)

Published in the journal *La Conque* of 1st June 1891.

L. 5 — *la courrière*: Littré notes that the feminine form of the word is chiefly used in poetry: "courrière" seems to be associated with the moon as "courier of the night", which connects with the imagery of reflected light in the Mallarmé poem.

Autre éventail de Mademoiselle Mallarmé (page 118)

Published in *La Revue critique* of 6th April 1884. The Barbier and Millan edition of the *Poésies* includes a facsimile of the poem as reprinted with an illustration by Albert Guillaume, in the *Gil Blas illustré* of 4th June 1892.[98]

L. 12-13 — *Ne peut jaillir ni s'apaiser. // Sens-tu le paradis farouche*: compare 'Toast Funèbre' lines 32-33: "Le Maître, par un œil profond, a, sur ses pas, / Apaisé de l'éden l'inquiète merveille".

Éventail de Méry Laurent (page 120)

Written 1890, and published posthumously in the 1945 *Œuvres complètes*.

L. 1-2 — *De frigides roses pour vivre / Toutes la même*: the poem was written in white ink on a gilded paper fan decorated with roses.[99] The roses are superimposed ("Toutes la même") when the fan is folded, and set free when it opens in the second quatrain.[100]

L. 5-6 — *que mon battement délivre / La touffe*: Roger Pearson[101] notes the similar passage in 'L'Après-midi d'un faune', line 82ff, where the faun has "divisé la

---

[98] It's worth knowing that Mallarmé's fan poems were made to be handwritten on real fans: Mademoiselle Mallarmé's fan is reproduced in the Mallarmé special issue of *Le Point*, XXIX-XXX, Fev-Av 1944, 55, and Madame Mallarmé's in Yves Peyré (ed.), *Mallarmé 1842-1898: Un destin d'écriture*, 19.

[99] *OC*, 1475.

[100] See Roger Pearson, *Mallarmé and Circumstance*, 198.

[101] *Mallarmé and Circumstance*, 203.

touffe échevelée / De baisers". The word "battement" occurs in all three éventail poems, and can also refer to the "beats" of a line of verse (Littré, *Battement* 7°).

L. 14 — *L'arôme émané de Méry*: Graham Robb[102] sees in "émané" an allusion to the painter Edouard Manet (Laurent and Mallarmé first met through their mutual friendship with Manet). The word also appears in another poem written for Méry, the sonnet "Ô si chère de loin et proche…"

Roger Pearson[103] notes that the four rhymes in *-ivre* are borrowed from "Le vierge, le vivace et le bel aujourd'hui…"

Feuillet d'album (page 122)

Published in *La Wallonie*, September-December 1892.

L. 9 — *ce vain souffle que j'exclus*: to "exclude the breath" with one's fingers is to block the flow of air by fingering the holes of the flute.[104] The verb also occurs in the sonnet "Toute l'âme résumée…", suggesting that a skilfully-smoked cigar is also a kind of wind instrument.

Remémoration d'amis belges (page 124)

Published in the anthology *Excelsior! 1883-1893* (Bruges, 1893). Mallarmé had visited Belgium in 1890 to deliver a memorial lecture on his friend Villiers de l'Isle-Adam.

L. 4 — *se dévêt pli selon pli la pierre veuve*: the stone is divesting itself at daybreak of veil after veil of incense-coloured fog.

L. 7 — *Nous immémoriaux quelques-uns si contents*: this line was enclosed in parentheses in the *Excelsior!* anthology.

L. 10 — *l'aube*: the first light of dawn, from Latin "albus" ("white"), echoed in (multiplied by) the whiteness of the swans.

---

[102] *Unlocking Mallarmé*, 82.
[103] *Mallarmé and Circumstance*, 203.
[104] A.R. Chisholm, 'Two Notes on Mallarmé', *Essays in French Literature*, vol. 7 (1970), 33-37, 35.

"Dame / sans trop d'ardeur à la fois enflammant…" (page 126)

Published in *Le Figaro* of 10th February 1896; not included in the 1899 *Poésies*.

L. 1-4 — These lines contain several echoes of Ronsard's 'À sa maistresse' ("Mignonne, allons voir si la rose…"),[105] and of Ronsard's ultimate source, the Latin poem "De rosis nascentibus" by Pseudo-Ausonius: both are classic statements of the urgency of gathering rosebuds, to which the forty-something Mallarmé seems to retort that there is no particular hurry.

L. 4 — *dans sa chair pleurer le diamant*: compare the similarly suggestive "Dans la considérable touffe / Expirer, comme un diamant" from "Quelle soie aux baumes de temps…"

L. 14 — *monotone*: the poem was written in 1887 for Méry Laurent. In a letter of February 1896, Mallarmé wrote, "For me, […] the sonnet […] would translate 'a need for calm friendship with neither crises of passion nor too robust a flame exhausting the flower of sentiment, this rose, etc'". Though Laurent always denied having had a physical relationship with Mallarmé,[106] some of the poems he wrote for her have an obvious (and occasionally quite barbed) sexual charge. I would link this poem to Mallarmé's gallant but excruciated letter to Laurent of 11th September 1889,[107] which Gordon Millan interprets as marking the point where Laurent terminated a physical affair — "monotone" does indeed imply calm friendship, but there's a definite implication of monotony there too.

"Ô si chère de loin et proche et blanche, si…" (page 128)

Written around 1886 and published posthumously in *La Phalange* of 15th January 1908.

---

[105] Ode XVII in *Le Premier livre des Odes*. Noted by Henry Weinfield, *Stéphane Mallarmé: Collected Poems*, 200.

[106] See Roger Pearson, *Stéphane Mallarmé*, 125.

[107] Quoted (in English translation) by Gordon Millan, *A Throw of the Dice: the Life of Stéphane Mallarmé*, 274.

"Rien, au réveil, que vous n'ayez..." (page 130)

Published in the journal *La Coupe* in June 1896; not collected in the 1899 *Poésies*. The earliest version of the poem dates from 1885.

L. 1 — *Rien*: by placing the word at the beginning of the refrain, where its meaning must shift to accommodate the surrounding syntax, Mallarmé emphasises the French word's tendency to vibrate between the senses of "nothing" and "anything".[108]

L. 6 — *Sans crainte*: probably a deliberate echo of "Sans craindre" in 'Salut' (which also begins with "Rien"; the phrase does not occur in the 1885 version of the rondel).

"Si tu veux nous nous aimerons..." (page 132)

Published in the journal *La Plume* of 15th March 1896; not collected in the 1899 *Poésies*.

The syntax of the first line/refrain echoes "À cette heure où nous nous taisons" from 'Prose (pour des Esseintes)': a theme of both poems is that the world, and love, go on existing independently of the human desire to speak of them.

Chansons bas (page 135)

Commissioned by the artist Jean-François Raffaelli to accompany his illustrations in the serially-published volume *Les Types de Paris*.[109] 'Le Vitrier' was not used,[110] and was first published in the *Poésies* of 1913. Only the two

---

[108] This tendency noted by Robert Greer Cohn, *Toward the poems of Mallarmé*, 33, with reference to *Salut*.

[109] Published by Plon, Nourrit et Cie for *Le Figaro*, 1889. See L.J. Austin, 'Mallarmé and the visual arts', *Poetic principles and practice*, 121-154.

[110] Probably because Raffaelli included a full-page drawing of a glazier in an earlier instalment of the book, to accompany a text by Edmond de Goncourt. Judging by the tiny thumbnail sketch included in Raffaelli's letter to Mallarmé of 28th August 1888 (reproduced in the Austin essay, p. 147), this was the drawing originally intended to go

sonnets, 'Le Savetier' and 'La Marchande d'herbes aromatiques', were included in the 1899 *Poésies*. Strictly speaking, 'Chansons bas' refers only to the two sonnets; the group title 'Types de la rue' ("Street characters") was given to the seven poems illustrated in *Les Types de Paris*. None of the illustrations were included in the 1899 *Poésies*.

Le Savetier (page 135)

L. 8 — *Un besoin de talons nus*: compare the "talon nu" in "M'introduire dans ton histoire…" and the "talons ingénus" of Venus in 'L'Après-midi d'un faune'.

La Marchande d'herbes aromatiques (page 137)

L. 6 — *lieux*: "les lieux d'aisances" = "loos".

Le Cantonnier (page 139)

L. 1 — *caillou*: "a stone or pebble hard enough to strike sparks from" (Littré), but also slang for "head". Also compare "Las de l'amer repos…": "De creuser par veillée une fosse nouvelle / Dans le terrain avare et froid de ma cervelle."

L. 1 — *nivelles*: "niveler" = "to level", but also an archaic verb meaning "to amuse oneself with trivial things" (Littré, *niveler* 2°).

Le Marchand d'ail et d'oignons (page 141)

L. 1 — *L'ennui d'aller en visite*: in a letter to Francis Coppée of 5th December 1866,[III] Mallarmé complained of the endless round of inane social "visites" which was expected of him after his move to Besançon.

Le Vitrier (page 145)

L. 1 — *Le pur soleil*: compare the "pur soleil mortel" of 'Toast Funèbre'. The glazier is carrying a rack of glass samples on his back, as in Baudelaire's prose

---

with Mallarmé's quatrain, and it is reproduced here on that assumption.
[III] *Correspondance*, 328.

poem 'Le Mauvais vitrier'.

Billet (page 150)

Written at Whistler's request and published under the title 'The Whirlwind' in the self-styled "lively and eccentric" (= very right-wing) English newspaper, *The Whirlwind*, on 15th November 1890.[112]

L. 9 — *tout, hormis lui, rebattu*: either "everything hackneyed, except the tutu", or "everything hackneyed, except Whistler".

L. 10 — *ivre, immobile*: these are also key terms in "Le vierge, le vivace et le bel aujourd'hui…", though the dancer seems more spirited than swanlike.

---

[112] An editorial in this issue, entitled "BROUHAHA", reads: "We need not offend our cultured readers' understanding by saying that, in offering for their delight an original sonnet by Stéphane Mallarmé, we are affording them a rare privilege.

To Monsieur Mallarmé, the chief of the "Décadents", is conceded the position of the most *vingtième siècle* poet in France, and to us has been granted the charming distinction of discovering, to the barbarians in these islands, this latest trill of that Singer.

For men whose education has been perfected and whose perceptions have been sharpened by a study of THE WHIRLWIND during now nearly five months, it is not necessary to place dots upon all the i's, — and for the rest, what matters it? Still, — filled with joy as we are, and in possession of supreme masterpieces, — this is a moment in which it is our humour to consider even the bewilderment of the outer Philistine. For his further stupefaction, then, it pleases us to tell him that, though the old verse of France was prosaically correct in its syntax, irreproachable in its conventionality, staid and chill in its essence, Art was unsatisfied. And, as to us, after an era of rampant *bourgeois* mediocrity, came Edgar Poe, so to France, after desperate academic dulness, came Beaudelaire [sic.], — and now Stéphane Mallarmé, who has affected a revolution in the dovecots of poetical orthodoxy. Colour, harmony, and musical effect alone bring with them that completeness, that polished finish, that correction, which accompany infallibly the work of the Master. These high verities are revealed only born with the Artist's power to apply them. This man is the *raffiné* Prince of "Décadents" — the classic of Modernity — Stéphane Mallarmé".

Mallarmé seems to have assumed that Whistler had a hand in the writing of the editorial (see C.P. Barbier (ed.), *Mallarmé-Whistler: Correspondance*, 76).

L. 12 — *se faire autrement de bile*: "se faire de la bile" is literally "to worry".

Petit air I (page 152)

Published as a facsimile of Mallarmé's handwriting, accompanied by a lithograph by Maurice Denis, in the journal *L'Épreuve* in November 1894 (reproduced as frontispiece to the Barbier and Millan edition of the *Poésies*). The translation attempts to follow Charles Mauron's interpretation,[113] in which "une solitude" (line 1) is the subject of both the verbs "mire" (line 3) and "longe" (line 9). The notes to the Marchal (ed.) *Poésies* outline several other possibilities.

Petit air II (page 154)

First published in the 1899 *Poésies*.

L. 7-8 — *L'oiseau qu'on n'ouït jamais / Une autre fois en la vie*: given its proximity to the swans in 'Petit air I' and "Le vierge, le vivace et le bel aujourd'hui...", perhaps an allusion to the swan's legendary death-song.[114] That its voice is followed by no echo, however, suggests that the hearer is the one who has actually died.

Petit air (guerrier) (page 156)

First published in *La Revue blanche* of 1st February 1895, as an epigraph to the essay 'L'Action' (collected in *Divagations* under the title 'L'action restreinte'). Mallarmé is rejecting the pressure exerted on him to write socially-committed literature.[115]

L. 1 — *Ce me va hormis l'y taire*: "It suits me, except to keep quiet about it", also, punningly, "Ce me va hors militaire" ("It suits me, outside the military").

PLUSIEURS SONNETS (page 158)

The section heading is usually taken to refer to the four untitled sonnets which

[113] *Mallarmé l'Obscur*, 109.
[114] Noted by Milner, *Mallarmé au tombeau*, 55.
[115] See Kevin O'Neill, 'Mallarmé's "Petit air (guerrier)"', *Studi Francesi*, vol. 16 (1972), 376-379, for more on the poem's origin.

immediately follow it — though, as Pascal Durand notes,[116] a reader of the 1899 *Poésies* (or indeed any of the early editions) would be as likely to take it for a descriptive title for the whole of the remainder of the book (which consists entirely of sonnets from this point on). The 1945 *Œuvres complètes* obscured the ambiguity by adding a further section heading, "Hommages et tombeaux", after the fourth sonnet.

"Quand l'ombre menaça de la fatale loi..." (page 158)

Published under the title 'Cette nuit' ("This night") in Verlaine's article on Mallarmé in the journal *Lutèce*, 24-30th November 1883. Malcolm Bowie's essay 'Genius at Nightfall: Mallarmé's "Quand l'ombre menaça de la fatale loi..."'[117] is a particularly good guide to the complex ambiguities of the poem's syntax.

L. 1 — *unalterable law*: stolen for the translation from George Meredith's poem 'Lucifer in Starlight'.[118]

L. 1-4 — the imagery of shadow, execution ("fatale loi"), vertebrae and folded wings is very close to that of the second stanza of the 'Cantique de saint Jean'.

L. 13 — *Roule dans cet ennui des feux vils*: the use of the verb "rouler" prefigures

---

[116] *Poésies de Stéphane Mallarmé*, 56.

[117] In Christopher Prendergast (ed.) *Nineteenth-Century French Poetry: Introductions to Close Reading*, 225-242.

[118] The Meredith poem was first published in 1883, too late to have influenced, or been influenced by, the Mallarmé, but the parallels are striking: wings, pride and shadow, the "rolling ball" of Earth, a royal personage sinking before the "starr'd night" (and the "lux" in Lucifer, bringer of light, is punningly present in Mallarmé's "Luxe"). Mallarmé and Meredith were to be favourably compared "for artistic aspiration, originality and independence of spirit" in Mme. Alphonse Daudet's *Notes sur Londres, Mai 1895* (see Henri Mondor et L.J. Austin (eds.), *Stéphane Mallarmé, Correspondance, IX, Jan-Nov 1897*, 125). Mondor and Austin also note the similarity between Mallarmé's conception of the poet's duty as "the orphic explication of the Earth" and the title of Meredith's 1888 collection *A Reading of Earth*. For Arthur Symons in *The Symbolist Movement in Literature*, 70, "Some of Meredith's poems, and occasional passages from his prose, can alone give in English some faint idea of the later prose and verse of Mallarmé."

the stars/dice rolled out by thought at the end of 'Un coup de Dés jamais n'abolira le Hasard'.

L. 13 — *cet ennui*: forming a minimal pair, phonologically, with "cette nuit" in line 9.

L. 14 — *un astre en fête*: E. Noulet[119] notes that in this poem, only the planet Earth merits the name "astre": the actual stars are only named by periphrasis, as "des guirlandes célèbres" or "des feux vils". Compare also the earthly "jardins de cet astre" in line 41 of 'Toast Funèbre'.[120]

"Le vierge, le vivace et le bel aujourd'hui..." (page 160)

Published March 1885 in *La Revue indépendante*.

L. 3 — *ce lac dur*: Jean-Claude Milner[121] sees a play on "lac" as an imaginary singular of "lacs" ("a snare").

L. 7 — *Pour n'avoir pas chanté la région où vivre*: note the solfège syllables "la ré" in "chanté *la ré*gion". The sonnet includes (orthographically or phonetically) all of the French solfège syllables, *do, ré, mi, fa, sol, la, si* (and the archaic *ut*), and "l'horreur du *sol*" could be taken as the revenge of the swan's unsung music.[122]

L. 10 — *l'oiseau qui le nie*: compare line 12 of the preceding poem, "Quand l'ombre menaça de la fatale loi...", where space denies itself, rather than waiting to be denied by a bird.

---

[119] *Vingt poèmes de Stéphane Mallarmé*, 91.

[120] 'Astre' can refer to anything in the sky, as in Mallarmé's prose poem 'Plainte d'automne', where the word is applied successively to a constellation, a star and a planet: "Ever since Maria left me to go to another star — which one, Orion, Altair, and you, green Venus? — I have always cherished solitude".

[121] *Mallarmé au tombeau*, 21.

[122] See Heath Lees, *Mallarmé and Wagner: Music and Poetic Language* for Mallarmé's deployment of solfège syllables in other works, including the prose poem 'Le Démon de l'analogie'. Lees notes that the eleventh century music theorist Guido d'Arezzo is reputed to have derived the solfège syllables from the words of 'Ut queant laxis', a plainchant hymn to John the Baptist (p. 29).

L. 13 — *Il s'immobilise au songe froid de mépris*: Milner[123] notes the distinction in Littré between the physiological implications of "songe" and "rêve": speech and/or movement are possible during the latter, but not the former. Milner also notes[124] the inverted parallel with Mallarmé's 'L'Azur': the speaker of that poem wants to put some clothes ("lambeaux") on "mépris", while here the "songe froid de mépris" is what clothes the exiled swan.

L. 14 — *le Cygne*: perhaps the constellation Cygnus. L.J. Austin[125] notes that the homophone "signe" also means "constellation", as in "les signes du Zodiaque". Compare also the line from Sonnet VI of Ronsard's *Derniers vers:* "Ma plume vole au Ciel pour estre quelque signe" ("My quill-pen flies to the Sky to be a sign").

"Victorieusement fui le suicide beau..." (page 162)

The earliest version, published in *Les Hommes d'aujourd'hui* in February 1887, is quite different:

> Toujours plus souriant au désastre plus beau,
> Soupirs de sang, or meurtrier, pâmoison, fête!
> Une millième fois avec ardeur s'apprête
> Mon solitaire amour à vaincre le tombeau.
>
> Quoi! de tout ce coucher pas même un cher lambeau
> Ne reste, il est minuit, dans la main du poète
> Excepté qu'un trésor trop folâtre de tête
> Y verse sa lueur diffuse sans flambeau!
>
> La tienne, si toujours frivole! c'est la tienne,
> Seul gage qui des soirs évanouis retienne
> Un peu de désolé combat en s'en coiffant

[123] *Mallarmé au tombeau*, 65; Littré, *songe*.
[124] *Mallarmé au tombeau*, 66.
[125] *Poetic principles and practice*, 216.

Avec grâce, quand sur des coussins tu la poses
Comme un casque guerrier d'impératrice enfant
Dont pour te figurer il tomberait des roses.

("Always more smiling on the most beautiful disaster,
sighs of blood, murderous gold, swoon, feasting!
a thousand times with ardour my solitary love
prepares itself to vanquish the tomb.

Why! of all this bedtime, not even one dear tatter
lingers, it is midnight, in the hand of the poet
except that a too playful treasure of the head
pours its diffuse glow there without a torch!

yours, frivolous as always! it is yours,
sole proof that holds back from the vanished evenings
a little contrite combat, doing up its hair

with grace, when you compose it upon cushions
like the battle helmet of an infant empress
from which, to stand for you, would tumble roses.") [126]

The definitive version of the poem was published only a few months later, in the *Poésies* of 1887).

L. 1 — the "suicide" is either that of the setting sun (in which case the first quatrain of the poem might be taken to be spoken by the sun itself),[127] or the temptation of suicide from which a human speaker flees.

---

[126] In line 5, *coucher* also = "sunset". Albert Sonnenfeld ('Eros and Poetry: Mallarmé's disappearing visions', in Beaumont, Cocking and Cruickshank (eds.), *Order and Adventure in Post-Romantic French Poetry*, 89-98) sees this early draft as an account of male masturbation.
[127] Gardner Davies, *Mallarmé et le drame solaire*, 83.

L. 2 — *sang par écume*: the association between sea-foam and bodily fluid goes back to Hesiod's account (*Theogony*, lines 173ff.) of the birth of Aphrodite from the white foam which spread out from the severed genitals of Ouranos, thrown into the sea after his castration by Kronos. [128]

"Ses purs ongles très haut dédiant leur onyx..." (page 164)

First published in the *Poésies* of 1887.

Here is the version of the earliest manuscript, dating from 1868:

Sonnet

allégorique de lui-même

La Nuit approbatrice allume les onyx
De ses ongles au pur Crime, lampadophore,
Du Soir aboli par le vespéral Phœnix
De qui la cendre n'a de cinéraire amphore

Sur des consoles, en le noir Salon: nul ptyx,
Insolite vaisseau d'inanité sonore,
Car le Maître est allé puiser de l'eau du Styx
Avec tous ses objets dont le Rêve s'honore.

Et selon la croisée au Nord vacante, un or
Néfaste incite pour son beau cadre une rixe

---

[128] Noted by Robert Greer Cohn, *Toward the Poems of Mallarmé*, 262. See also my notes to "Mes bouquins refermés sur le nom de Paphos…" Charles Bernstein's homophonic translation of Mallarmé's 'Salut' (as 'Salute', in *My Way: Speeches and Poems*, 12) opens, "Nothing, this cum, verging verse". The word "Meerschaum" ("écume de mer" in French), the name of a kind of soft white stone often used to make the bowls of tobacco pipes, unites two of Mallarmé's key symbols, sea-foam and smoke: the exhibition catalogue *Mallarmé et les "Siens"* (Musée de Sens, 1998, p. 125) includes a photograph of Mallarmé's Meerschaum pipe.

Faite d'un dieu que croit emporter une nixe

En l'obscurcissement de la glace, décor
De l'absence, sinon que sur la glace encor
De scintillations le septuor se fixe.

("Sonnet

allegorical of itself

Approving night lights up the onyx
of its fingernails at the pure Crime, lampadephore,
of the Evening abolished by the vesperal Phœnix
whose ashes have no cinerary amphora

on consoles, in the black Salon: no ptyx,
unwonted vessel of sonorous inanity,
for the Master has gone to draw water from the Styx
with all his objects on which the Dream prides itself.

And along with the cross-pane vacant to the north, a fatal
gold incites for its fine frame a brawl
caused by a god a nixe thinks to carry off

into the darkening of the mirror, Décor
of absence, except that, on the mirror again
the septet of scintillations settles in.")[129]

---

[129] Note that the early version has one more rhyme in —*yx(e)* than the poem as published. The 'Sonnet allégorique' seems to have enjoyed unusual celebrity for an unpublished poem: an 1875 article by Adolphe Racot (quoted in the Barbier and Millan *Poésies*, 222) gives Mallarmé's reply to the poet Leconte de Lisle, who, after hearing Mallarmé recite the poem, had asked if the "ptyx" was meant to be a piano: "Not at all, my dear master, he replied with candour. I just needed a rhyme for Styx;

L. 1 — *ongles ... onyx*: "onyx" is from a Greek word meaning "fingernail", "horn" or "hoof". Compare the sky that burns on the fingernail raised in the 'Ouverture ancienne d'Hérodiade', lines 822ff.

L. 2 — *lampadophore*: "torch-bearer" — a rare French word corresponding to the rare English word "lampadephore". It seemed better, as with "ptyx", not to domesticate the word with a paraphrase: the strangeness of the word-choice is a large part of the poem's point.

L. 3 — *le Phénix*: Graham Robb[130] relates this to the constellation Phœnix, a southern counterpart of the "septuor" of Ursa Major. It might be worth noting that Phœnix is placed in the sky next to the constellation Eridanus, named for a river located by the ancients either in the underworld (like the Styx) or somewhere in northern Europe. Apollonius Rhodius[131] describes how Phaeton fell burning into Eridanus, and ever since then, no bird can cross the river without plunging into the fire.

L. 5 — *ptyx*: not a word in either French or English, but the root means "fold" in Greek.[132] Graham Robb[133] notes that a "ptyx" can be a waxed wooden writing tablet (one half of a *diptych*) — in this light, the "Aboli bibelot d'inanité sonore" would be the poem itself, along with its physical substrate, and the poem, in recursively containing both, really would be a "Sonnet allegorical of

---

not finding any, I created a new musical instrument: and yet, it is clear, the ptyx is unwonted, because there is no such thing; it resonates well, because it rhymes; and it is no less a vessel of inanity, because it has never existed!" Patrick McGuinness ("'Beaucoup de bruit pour rien': Mallarmé's "ptyx" and the Symbolist "bric-a-brac"', *The Romanic Review* vol. 86 no. 1 (1995), 103-113) notes an 1885 article by Anatole France which also alludes to Mallarmé's "Ptyx".

[130] 'The Phoenix of Mallarmé's "Sonnet en –yx"', *French Studies Bulletin,* vol. 7 no. 24, (Autumn 1987), 13-15.

[131] *Argonautica*, Book IV, lines 592ff.

[132] *Poésies* ed. Marchal, 242.

[133] *Unlocking Mallarmé*, 63.

itself". By contrast, E. Noulet[134] quotes from the *Thesaurus linguae grecae* which defines "πτυχάς" as an oyster shell. The 'Sonnet allégorique' calls the "ptyx" a "vessel", and in the final version the "ptyx" seems to be the object used by the Master to draw up the tears: "writing tablet" and "oyster shell" would both be fit for purpose, figuratively and slightly-less figuratively. Ultimately, the poem provides its own definition: the "ptyx" is an "abolished bauble of sonorous inanity", an empty signifier with beautiful plumage.[135]

L. 7 — *puiser*: "to draw or dip", perhaps an echo of the American English "big dipper" for the seven bright stars of Ursa Major (the "septuor" of line 14).[136]

L. 11 — *une nixe*: a nixe or nixie, a female Germanic water-spirit. "Like the sirens, the nixe by her song draws listening youth to herself, and then into the deep"[137] — with the difference that sirens don't live in the water. Lorelei and

---

[134] *L'Œuvre poétique de Stéphane Mallarmé*, 454.

[135] One last go: Nikolaj d'Origny Lübecker (*Le sacrifice de la sirène: Un coup de dés et la poétique de Stéphane Mallarmé*, 88 n. 2) notes that, according to Pausanias (*Description of Greece*, 8.18.6), the only object which can hold the immensely corrosive water of the Styx is a horse's hoof. Pausanias repeats an ancient rumour that Alexander the Great was poisoned by Styx-water brought to him in a hoof. The Mallarmé sonnet has hooves at the beginning (in the etymology of "ongles" and "onyx") and at the end (what the unicorns kick with), with a suggestion of poisoning in the middle (one historical meaning of "crédence", noted by Pearson, *Unfolding Mallarmé*, 161, is a table on which food and drink were laid out to be tasted by servants before the master's meal). "Ptyx" doesn't mean "hoof", though, and it's probably going too far to hear a phonetic approximation of the French "sabot" hidden in "pty**x**, / **Abo**li". Perhaps the oysters were contaminated.

[136] See Robert Greer Cohn, *Toward the Poems of Mallarmé* 146 n.4. The common French names for this asterism are "le Chariot" and "la Casserole".

[137] Jacob Grimm, *Teutonic Mythology* (tr. James Steven Stallybrass), volume 2, 492. Given the speculation about the 'ptyx', it might be worth noting the names of two shellfish listed in Grimm's book (p.489): the Swedish 'näcköra' (="nix-ear") or abalone, and the Finnish 'näkinkenka' (="nix-shoe") or pearl-mussel. Grimm also notes two botanical nixes which have Mallarméan associations: the Finnish 'näkin waltikka'

Wagner's Rhine maidens were nixes, and there is another in Baudelaire's poem 'L'Avertisseur'.

L. 12 — *défunte nue*: if the "nue" isn't a cloud reflected in the mirror, then it's more likely to be the adjective "naked" than the noun "female nude" (a naked, dead-woman rather than a dead, naked-woman: L.J. Austin[138] notes that "nue" is not normally used as a noun in this sense). The line recalls the reflected naked phantom in Mallarmé's prose poem 'Frisson d'hiver' (see the notes to 'Scène: Hérodiade'). E. Noulet's interpretation of the final tercet,[139] which takes "Elle", rather than "le septuor" as the subject of "se fixe", visualising the nixe as being fixed in place (as if by nails) *by* the septet of stars, is tempting, though it would seem to stretch the syntax of line 14 a little. The verblessness of line 12 is, in any case, very close to that of line 13 of 'Le Tombeau de Charles Baudelaire', "Celle son Ombre même un poison tutélaire", so it's probably the septuor that's installing itself in oblivion.

I suspect that Marcel Duchamp's late installation work *Étant donnés* (1946-1966, in the Philadelphia Museum of Art) might be, in part, an attempt at a literal visualisation of the Mallarmé sonnet: it has a lamp-bearer, an apparently "défunte nue" associated with water, involves the experience of looking into one framed but ambiguous space from another,[140] even a "ptyx" (if one takes "ptyx" to mean

---

(="nix-sceptre") or bulrush, and the German 'Nix-blume' or water-lily.

[138] *Poetic principles and practice*, 197 n.17.

[139] *Vingt poèmes de Stéphane Mallarmé*, 190f. A.S. Kline's translation of the poem (online at www.brindin.com) seems to follow Noulet's interpretation.

[140] See Mallarmé's letter to Henri Cazalis of 18th July 1868, describing the kind of illustration that might be made to accompany the 'Sonnet allégorique': "For example, a window open at night, the two shutters fastened; a room with no-one in it, despite the air of solidity presented by the fastened shutters, and, in a night made of absence and questioning, with no furniture apart from the plausible suggestion of vague console tables, a bellicose and dying mirror-frame hung on the back wall, with its reflection, stellar and incomprehensible, of the Great Bear, which links this dwelling, abandoned by the world, to the sky alone." (*Correspondance*, 392). The shutters are described as "attachés", probably "fastened back against the wall" rather than "fastened shut", but

"oyster shell" and uses the last line of "Une negresse…" as an intertext).[141] The backdrop of *Étant donnés* is a hand-coloured photograph of a ravine near the Swiss town of Puidoux[142] — the visual pun on the lady's ptyx is also a verbal one, given the Greek figurative sense of "ptyx" as "a mountain-cleft, vale or ravine".[143] Finally, the "Maître" is absent from *Étant donnés* because it was conceived as a posthumous work, only to be exhibited after Duchamp's death.

L. 14 — *le septuor*: in Edgar Allan Poe's prose dialogue "The Power of Words", the seven stars of the Pleiades also make stellar music: "Come! we will leave to the left the loud harmony of the Pleiades…"

"Sur les bois oubliés quand passe l'hiver sombre…" (page 166)

Published posthumously in the *Poésies* of 1913. The poem is thought to have been written in memory of Ettie Maspéro, the wife of the Egyptologist Gaston Maspéro. Cecily Mackworth[144] notes that Maspéro became interested in spiritualism after Ettie's death, and confided his interest to Mallarmé.

The poem has strong echoes[145] of Baudelaire's "La servante au grand cœur…" written in memory of Mariette, the servant of his childhood home. Baudelaire's

---

the phrasing seems ambiguous enough to find an echo in *Étant donnés*, which can only be viewed through two tiny peep-holes in a pair of closed wooden doors.

[141] Charles Mauron, *Introduction to the Psychoanalysis of Mallarmé*, 143 also puts a sexual spin on "ptyx".

[142] Gavin Parkinson, *The Duchamp Book*, 84; see also p.179 n. 20.

[143] Georg Autenrieth, *An Homeric Dictionary*, online at http://www.perseus.tufts.edu/hopper/. This is the Greek meaning which underlies Victor Hugo's use of "Ptyx" in his poem 'Le Satyre': "…on entendait Chrysis / Sylvain du Ptyx que l'homme appelle Janicule" (noted by E. Noulet, *L'Œuvre poétique de Stéphane Mallarmé*, 454). Michael Riffaterre (*Semiotics of Poetry*, 18) counters that Hugo's "Ptyx" is meant to be the name of a real mountain translated into the language of the gods, and thus a word with no meaning in any human language.

[144] *English Interludes*, 33. Mackworth describes a contemporary photograph of a séance in which (a known drawing of) Ettie appears in the ectoplasm.

[145] Noted by Wallace Fowlie, *Mallarmé*, 184.

poem regrets the untended flowers on Mariette's grave, and ends:

> Lorsque la bûche siffle et chante, si le soir,
> Calme, dans le fauteuil je la voyais s'asseoir,
> Si, par une nuit bleue et froide de décembre,
> Je la trouvais tapie en un coin de ma chambre,
> Grave, et venant du fond de son lit éternel
> Couver l'enfant grandi de son œil maternel,
> Que pourrais-je répondre à cette âme pieuse,
> Voyant tomber des pleurs de sa paupière creuse?

("If, on an evening when the hearth-log whistles and sings, / I saw her sit down calmly in an armchair, / if, on a blue and cold December night, / I found her hidden in a corner of my room, / gravely come forth from the depths of her eternal bed / to brood with a maternal eye over the grown-up child, / what answer would I give that pious soul, / seeing tears fall from her hollow eyelid?")

Le Tombeau d'Edgar Poe (page 168)

Published in *E. Allan Poe. A Memorial Volume* (Baltimore, 1877).

L. 5 — *un vil sursaut d'hydre*: Roger Pearson[146] notes that a hydra is a water-monster, standing for the insults thrown at Poe by tee-totallers.

L. 9 — *grief*: literally "grievance". Mallarmé's own English translation of a slightly earlier version of the sonnet[147] translates "grief" as "struggle".

---

[146] *Mallarmé and Circumstance*, 167.
[147] Included (with Mallarmé's own numbered annotations) in a letter of 31st July 1877 (*Correspondance*, 563) to the American poet Sarah Helen Whitman (1803-1878), who had once been engaged to marry Poe:

> "Such as into himself at last Eternity changes him,
> The Poet arouses with a naked (1) hymn
> His century overawed not to have known
> That death extolled itself in this (2) strange voice:

L. 10 — *un bas-relief:* Poe's monument in Baltimore originally featured a marble bas-relief portrait of the poet. [148]

L. 12 — *Calme bloc:* in the 'Scolies' to his translation of Poe's poems, Mallarmé wrote: "I will never cease to admire the practical means by which these people, inconvenienced by so much unsolveable mystery emanating forever from the corner of earth where, for a quarter century, the corpse of Poe lay abandoned, have, under the cover of a useless and belated tomb, rolled a stone there, immense, formless, heavy, deprecatory, as if to block up completely the place from which would exhale towards the sky, like a pestilence, the rightful claim of a Poet's existence forbidden by all". [149]

But, in a vile writhing of an hydra, (they) once hearing the Angel (3)
To give (4) too pure a meaning to the words of the tribe,
They (between themselves) thought (by him) the spell drunk
In the honourless flood of some dark mixture (5).

Of the soil and the ether (which are) enemies, o struggle!
If with it my idea does not carve a bas-relief
Of which Poe's dazzling (6) tomb be adorned,

(A) stern block here fallen from a mysterious disaster,
Let this granite at least show forever their bound
To the old flights of Blasphemy (still) spread in the future (7).

(1) Naked hymn means when the words take in death their absolute value.
(2) This means his own.
(3) The Angel means the above said Poet.
(4) To give means giving.
(5) Means in plain prose: charged him with always being drunk.
(6) Dazzling means with the idea of such a bas-relief.
(7) Blasphemy means against Poets, such as the charge of Poe being drunk."

Whitman's own "free imitation" in English of the Mallarmé poem is given in *OC,* 224.

[148] See the website of the Edgar Allan Poe Society of Baltimore, http://www.eapoe.org/balt/poegrave.htm

[149] *OC,* 226.

Le Tombeau de Charles Baudelaire (page 170)

Published in *La Plume* of 1st January 1895.

Baudelaire's poem 'Le Mort Joyeux' is not encouraging: "Je hais les testaments et je hais les tombeaux" ("I hate testaments and I hate tombs [*or* memorial poems]").

L. 4 — *Tout le museau*: a similar focus on the "whole" of a mere part of the body occurs in line 9 of "Le vierge, le vivace et le bel aujourd'hui...": "Tout son col".

L. 5 — *Ou que le gaz récent torde la mèche louche*: Paris had been lit by gas since 1820, but as L.J. Austin puts it,[150] "[it] was new for Baudelaire and an aspect of his modernity". Some commentators, including E. Noulet,[151] have seen in "le gaz récent" a reference to the "bec Auer", a new kind of gas-lamp introduced to Paris in the early 1890s, whose phallic form (a vertical glass tube) would then be the "immortel pubis" of line 7.[152] Jean Pommier[153] objects that "pubis" doesn't mean "penis", and quotes a letter from M.G. Combet, Directeur Général du Gaz de France, pointing out that gas lamps don't have wicks. "Mèche" can mean "a lock of hair" as well as "a wick", and both senses seem to be fully intended here: in the latter sense, the line would have to do with the victory of harsh, modern gaslight over the older, less revealing light of oil lamps.[154] In the former, it would be the hair on the "immortel pubis" of the Baudelairean figure of a prostitute, kept up, or out, as long as the street lamp is lit.[155]

---

[150] *Poetic principles and practice*, 178.

[151] *L'Œuvre poétique de Stéphane Mallarmé*, 471.

[152] "Le bec Auer" plays a phallic role in at least three works by Marcel Duchamp, including *Étant donnés*.

[153] *Dialogues avec le passé: études et portraits littéraires*, 185.

[154] Gardner Davies, *Les "Tombeaux" de Mallarmé*, 171. L.J. Austin (*Poetic principles and practice*, 178) sees a straightforward visual comparison between the gas-flame, contorted by the wind, and a lock of hair (inverting the terms of the metaphor in the first line of "La chevelure vol d'une flamme...") — though, given the context, the primary meaning of "mèche" as "wick" might tend to interfere with the image.

[155] For A.R. Chisholm (*Mallarmé's grand œuvre*, 22), "le gaz récent" means that the lamp has only just been lit. Peter Hambly ("Le Tombeau de Charles Baudelaire", in Jill

L. 6 — *Essuyeuse*: "une essuyeuse de plâtres" was a 19th century slang term for a prostitute.[156]

L. 7 — *un immortel pubis*: Gardner Davies[157] sees this as a reference to "the oldest profession".

L. 8 — *découche*: literally, "sleeps away from home".[158]

L. 9 — *sans soir*: deprived of evening by artificial light. The phrase also occurs in the earliest version of 'Les Fleurs' ("À jamais hosannah dans l'or des jours sans soirs"), and compare the "Soir aboli" of the 'Sonnet allégorique' and the "soirs évanouis" of the first version of "Victorieusement fui…" In line 5, "louche" can't possibly be a noun, but given the presence of The Big Dipper in "Ses purs ongles très haut dédiant leur onyx…" (and in 'Un coup de Dès jamais n'abolira le Hasard'), it might hold an echo of the feminine noun "louche", meaning "a ladle, or dipper": the stars would then be among the things abolished by gaslight.

L. 10 — *elle*: ambiguously "she" or "it"; the feminine pronoun refers back to "la mèche louche" (perhaps also to "idole" in line 3) and forward to "son Ombre".

Anderson (ed.), *Australian Divagations: Mallarmé & the 20th Century*, 230-252, 238) quotes Théodore de Banville: "As soon as the gas is lit, and the shops light up, on every pavement of the town… tall girls slip into the light, like spectres …tired of smiling and always smiling".

[156] Théophile Gautier (quoted in the definition of "Lorette" in Lorédan Larchey, *Les Excentricités du langage*, 193) explains that when one of the quartiers of Paris was under construction, the newly-built houses were rented out cheaply to make the area look lived-in. Many of the first tenants were prostitutes, who became known as "essuyeuses de plâtres", presumably "drying the plaster" with the heat of their exertions. Albert Barrère (*Argot and Slang*, 135) defines "essuyer les plâtres" as "to kiss the face of a female whose cheeks are painted". "La mèche… Essuyeuse" also recalls the women in Luke 7:38 and John 12:3 who wipe the feet of Jesus with their hair.

[157] *Les "Tombeaux" de Mallarmé*, 173.

[158] *Les "Tombeaux" de Mallarmé*, 175.

L. 12 — *Au voile qui la ceint absente avec frissons*: presumably the flame fluttering within its glass windshield; also an echo of the girdles ("ceintures") removed by the faun's art in line 56 of 'L'Après-midi d'un faune'.

L. 13 — *un poison tutélaire*: compare Baudelaire, 'Le Voyage' VIII: "Verse-nous ton poison pour qu'il nous réconforte!" ("Pour us your poison that it might strengthen us!") "Mallarmé is alluding to an influence not morally harmful, but poetically perilous, not in the quality of the influence, but in its strength. He remembers that in imitating Baudelaire, he almost lost his own originality".[159] Roger Pearson[160] simply notes that gas is poisonous, but sheds light.

Gérard de Nerval's poem 'Horus' (from *Les Chimères*) shares the Egyptian imagery and has an almost identical set of rhymes in —*ouche*.

Tombeau ("Le noir roc courroucé que la bise le roule…") (page 172)

Written shortly after Paul Verlaine's death in January 1896, and published in *La Revue blanche* of 1st January 1897.

L. 4 — *quelque funeste moule*: E. Noulet[161] notes that Mallarmé had been present when Verlaine's death-mask was taken, and was profoundly upset by the experience.

L. 6-7 — *Cet immatériel deuil … / … Nubiles plis*: "deuil" here is primarily "mourning-cloth". The folds of birdsong/cloth are presumably "nubile" because however mournful it might sound to humans, the bird's cooing is really a mating-call.[162]

L. 13-14 — *haleine … / … mort*: the inexorability with which the last two lines rhyme *in English* creates an echo of the English or Shakespearean sonnet, with its concluding couplet: both Mallarmé and Verlaine were teachers of English.[163]

[159] E. Noulet, *L'Œuvre poétique de Stéphane Mallarmé*, 473.
[160] "'Un peu profond ruisseau calomnié': Mallarmé and the Circumscription of Death', in Kinloch and Millan (eds.), *Situating Mallarmé*, 83-102, 86.
[161] *Vingt poèmes de Stéphane Mallarmé*, 261.
[162] Gardner Davies, *Les "Tombeaux" de Mallarmé*, 206.
[163] See Mallarmé's letter 'Sur Verlaine Professeur d'Anglais', in the Marchal (ed.) *OC*,

L. 14 — *Un peu profond ruisseau*: "le ruisseau" can also be the gutter.[164]

Hommage ("Le silence déjà funèbre d'une moire…") (page 174)

Published in *La Revue wagnérienne* of 8th January 1886. In a letter to his uncle, Paul Mathieu, Mallarmé wrote: "The 'Homage' is a little sullen; it is, as you will see, rather the melancholy of a poet who sees the old poetic confrontation collapse, and the magnificence of words fade, before the sunrise of contemporary Music, of which Wagner is the latest God".[165] *Divagations* includes a long essay, 'Richard Wagner: rêverie d'un poëte français', which has numerous points of connection with the 'Hommage'.

L. 3 — *du principal pilier*: L.J. Austin[166] sees this as a reference to Victor Hugo, a pillar of the old poetic (and theatrical) establishment, who died on Wagner's birthday, 22nd May 1885.

L. 6 — *Hiéroglyphes dont s'exalte le millier*: Mallarmé's very early essay 'Hérésies artistiques. L'Art pour tous' (1862) regrets that poetry is written in an everyday script accessible to ignorant and hostile readers, while a musical score repels the casual browser, "seized by a religious astonishment at the sight of those macabre processions of austere signs, chaste and unknown".[167] The line could also be translated "Hieroglyphs exalting by the thousand".

L. 14 — *Mal tu par l'encre même*: even reduced to a written score, Wagner's music is unsilenceable.

Hommage ("Toute Aurore même gourde…") (page 176)

Published 15th Janaury 1895 in an issue of *La Plume* devoted to the painter Pierre Puvis de Chavannes. Puvis painted a famous *Beheading of St. John the*

---

tome 2, 666.

[164] F.C. St. Aubyn, *Stéphane Mallarmé*, 101.

[165] *Correspondance*, 580 n. 3.

[166] *Essais Sur Mallarmé*, 39.

[167] Noted by L.J. Austin, *Essais sur Mallarmé*, 56.

Baptist (one version of which is in the National Gallery, London).

L. 5-6 — *la gourde / Jointe au bâton frappant dur*: Roger Pearson[168] notes the allusion to Exodus 17:6: "Behold, I will stand before thee there upon the rock in Horeb; and thou shalt smite the rock, and there shall come water out of it, that the people may drink". The same biblical passage is alluded to in Baudelaire's poem 'L'Héautontimorouménos' ("The one who torments himself"):

> Je te frapperai sans colère
> Et sans haine, comme un boucher,
> Comme Moïse le rocher!

("I will strike you without anger / and without hate, like a butcher, / as Moses struck the rock!")

L. 9 — *tu vis*: "vis" is either the present indicative of "vivre" ("to live") or the past historic of "voir" ("to see").[169]

"Au seul souci de voyager…" (page 178)

Probably the last poem Mallarmé finished: first published as a facsimile of Mallarmé's handwriting in *Album commémoratif A Vasco da Gama* (Lisbon/Paris, April 1898), an album of verse, prose, artwork and music commemorating the 400th anniversary of Vasco's voyage to India. The text given here is that of the album, which differs from that in the 1899 edition of the *Poésies* (which has line 3, "Ce salut soit le messager" and line 8, "Un oiseau d'annonce nouvelle"). Mallarmé did not include the poem in his own list of contents for the projected volume, and it seems to have been added posthumously by his daughter Geneviève, who used an early draft for copy-text.[170]

L. 7-8 — *Écumait toujours en ébats / Un oiseau d'ivresse nouvelle*: compare 'Brise

---

[168] *Mallarmé and Circumstance*, 218.

[169] *Mallarmé and Circumstance*, 220; the phrase "tu vis" also occurs in line 1 of 'Scène: Hérodiade'.

[170] See *Poésies*, ed. Barbier and Millan, 447.

marine': "Je sens que des oiseaux sont ivres / D'être parmi l'écume inconnue et les cieux!"[171]

L. 11 — *gisement*: either a nautical bearing, or a mineral deposit.[172]

"Toute l'âme résumée..." (page 180)

Published in the literary supplement to *Le Figaro*, 3rd August 1895, to accompany an interview with Mallarmé on the subject of *vers libre*. Not collected in the 1899 *Poésies*. As F.C. St. Aubyn notes,[173] the sonnet has about it a strong air of "fumisterie": art as hoax, as smokescreen.

L. 6 — *Brûlant savamment*: Mallarmé more than once implied that smoking required more of his skill than the writing of letters. His daughter Geneviève reports his advice to her on the posthumous publication of his letters: "if you allowed it to be done, I would come forth from my tomb, for, whenever I am incapable even of smoking a cigarette, I write a letter."[174]

L. 13 — *Le sens trop précis rature*: it might be worth remembering that Mallarmé went to school, and briefly worked in the Registry Office, in a town called "Sens". His autobiographical letter to Verlaine tells of having his early notebooks of verse repeatedly confiscated, presumably at the lycée in Sens.[175]

L. 13-14 — *rature (...) littérature*: the rhyme seems to have been borrowed from Theodore de Banville.[176] A very similar wordplay, "Lits et Ratures" ("Beds

---

[171] Noted by A.R. Chisholm, 'Mallarmé's Vasco Sonnet', *French Studies,* vol. 20 (1966), 139-143, 142.

[172] F.C. St. Aubyn, *Stéphane Mallarmé,* 105.

[173] *Stéphane Mallarmé,* 105.

[174] Geneviève Bonniot-Mallarmé, 'Mallarmé par sa fille', *La Nouvelle revue française,* 158, (1st November 1926), 517-523, 518. See also 'Pour ou contre le tabac', in the Marchal (ed.) *OC,* tome 2, 658.

[175] *OC,* 662.

[176] Eileen Souffrin-Le-Breton, 'A Mallarmé sonnet and the late poetry of Banville', *French Studies Bulletin,* vol. 19 no. 69 (Winter 1998), 4-7. A note appended to the

and Erasures" or, homophonically, "Lisez Ratures!", an injunction to "Read the Erasures!"), appears as part of Francis Picabia's cover image for the 1st December 1922 issue of the proto-Surrealist journal *Littérature*. The phrase itself is Marcel Duchamp's.[177]

L. 14 — *ta vague littérature* — E. Noulet[178] characterises "vague" as a synonym of "veiled, shadowy, misty, mysterious" rather than simply meaning "vague".

"Tout Orgueil fume-t-il du soir…" (page 182)

This, and the following two poems, published (alongside "Mes bouquins refermés sur le nom de Paphos…") in *La Revue indépendante* in January 1887. The group of three numbered octosyllabic sonnets is usually known as Mallarmé's "Triptych".

L. 3 — *l'immortelle bouffée*: "bouffée" can also refer back to "orgueil", implying "a fit of pride".

L. 4 — *Ne puisse à l'abandon surseoir*: the only other use in the *Poésies* of the whistling subjunctive "puisse" is in the final couplet of the 'Billet' to Whistler, where it also refers to a gust of air.

L. 8 — *S'il survenait par le couloir*: the "couloir" (a corridor or hallway) as a passage through which the dead might return recalls the "magique espoir du corridor" dismissed in 'Toast funèbre'.

L. 14 — *la fulgurante console*: a "console table", a kind of table supported by brackets fixed to a wall, with a suggestion of the verb "consoler":[179] the console

---

original interview described the verses as "banvillesquement rimés" (see the Marchal (ed). *OC*, tome 2, 712).

[177] Gavin Parkinson, *The Duchamp Book*, 156. See also Stephen Jay Gould, 'The Substantial Ghost: Towards a General Exegesis of Duchamp's Artful Wordplays', *toutfait: the Marcel Duchamp Studies Online Journal*, vol. 1, issue 2, May 2000 (online at www.toutfait.com).

[178] *Vingt poèmes de Stéphane Mallarmé*, 254.

[179] See Roger Pearson, *Unfolding Mallarmé*, 202.

table, shining as if lit by lightning, is a consolation for the absence of any other source of warmth, or life, in the room. A number of other Mallarmé poems (including 'Apparition,' "Quand l'ombre menaça…", "Ses purs ongles…", "M'introduire dans ton histoire…" and 'Un coup de Dés jamais n'abolira le Hasard') also end on an image of consolatory celestial light.

"Surgi de la croupe et du bond…" (page 184)

The imagery of rose, interruption, sylph and kiss is very close to that of Mallarmé's rondel ("Si tu veux nous nous aimerons…"), though in the sonnet the kiss never takes place, and the rose is never born.

L. 8 — *sylphe*: in alchemy, a mortal, soulless being inhabiting air. The desire, unfulfilled at the end of the poem, that the vessel might "breathe out anything announcing a rose in darkness", could also be taken for the sylph's desire for a soul (given the etymological link between soul [French "âme"] and breath [Latin "anima"], a link which is explicitly made in the first quatrain of "Toute l'âme résumée…") "Expirer" means both "to breathe out" and "to breathe one's last".

"Une dentelle s'abolit…" (page 186)

L. 4 — *absence éternelle de lit*: Mallarmé suffered from severe insomnia in later life.[180] For Charles Chadwick,[181] the contrast here is between the absence of any possible place of birth in the room (the bed as child-bed), and the musical instrument that sleeps in (or with) the poet ("chez qui du rêve se dore"), whose hollow belly (or perhaps that of the billowing lace curtain) might at least potentially have functioned as a womb. Mallarmé seems to be trying to visualise a mechanism for the kind of male motherhood first imagined in 'Don du poème'.[182]

---

[180] At one stage he claimed to have had only a single night's sleep in twelve years (Henri Mondor, *Vie de Mallarmé*, 735).

[181] *The Meaning of Mallarmé*, 71.

[182] See Barbara Johnson, 'Mallarmé as Mother', in *A World of Difference*, 137-143.

The movement in the Triptych as a whole seems to be:

1. an affirmation that death is absolutely final, and human pride only so much smoke;
2. an expression of doubt about the generative potential of physical love;
3. a very tentative positive statement about the creative power of art.

The mood of the Triptych has been linked[183] to the death in 1879 of Mallarmé's eight-year-old son Anatole, though the date of composition of the poems remains unknown.

"Quelle soie aux baumes de temps…" (page 188)

Published in *La Revue indépendante* in March 1885. A.R. Chisholm notes that the poem has a similar theme to that of 'Le Pitre châtié': the lover's sensual enjoyment would not be complete unless he were prepared to stifle the cry of "les Gloires" — art, idealism and genius.[184]

L. 3 — *la torse*: less gallantly, this can also be a feminine noun meaning "the action of twisting the silk being passed through a bath of dye" (Littré).

L. 12 — *la considérable touffe*: the "sidér" in "considérable"[185] suggests an astral association for the hair: either a comet (as in 'Scene: Hérodiade' l. 52f.), or the constellation Coma Berenices ("Berenice's Hair").

The earliest version, dating from 1868, is so different as to constitute a distinct poem:

Another "male mother", Pygmalion, appears in the notes (below) to "Mes bouquins refermés sur le nom de Paphos…"

[183] See (among others) André Vial, *Mallarmé: Tétralogie pour un enfant mort*, and Robert Greer Cohn, *Toward the Poems of Mallarmé*, 216.

[184] A.R. Chisholm, 'Mallarmé's Edens', part one, *AUMLA*, 13 (1960), 3-22, 9. Part two of the essay is in *AUMLA*, 14 (1960) 3-22.

[185] Etymology noted by Robert Greer Cohn, *Toward the Poems of Mallarme*, 220.

De l'orient passé des Temps
Nulle étoffe jadis venue
Ne vaut la chevelure nue
Que loin des bijoux tu détends.

Moi, qui vis parmi les tentures
Pour ne pas voir le Néant seul,
Mes yeux, las de ces sépultures,
Aimeraient ce divin linceul.

Mais tandis que les rideaux vagues
Cachent des ténèbres les vagues
Mortes, hélas! ces beaux cheveux

Lumineux en l'esprit font naître
D'atroces étincelles d'Être,
Mon horreur et mes désaveux.

("No fabric come forth long ago
from the outworn orient of Time
is worth the undressed hair
you set loose, far from all jewels.

I, who live among tapestries
so as not see Nothing alone,
my eyes, tired of these burials,
would love that divine shroud.

But while vague curtains
hide the waves of darkness
— dead, alas! this radiant hair

brings towards birth in the mind
atrocious sparks of Being,
my horror and all I deny.")

A second version dates from 1869:

Alternative

De l'oubli magique venue,
Nulle étoffe, musique et temps,
Ne vaut la chevelure nue
Que, loin des bijoux, tu détends.

En mon rêve, antique avenue
De tentures, seul, si j'entends
Le Néant, cette chère nue
Enfouira mes yeux contents!

Non. Comme par les rideaux vagues
Se heurtent du vide les vagues,
Pour un fantôme les cheveux

Font luxueusement renaître
La lueur parjure de l'Être,
— Son horreur et ses désaveux.

("Alternative

Brought forth from magical oblivion,
no fabric, music and time,
is worth the undressed hair
you set loose, far from all jewels.

If in my dream, that antique avenue
of tapestries, alone, I hear
Nothingness, that beloved cloud
will bury my happy eyes!

No. As waves of the void
clash through vague curtains,
for a phantom, all this hair

luxuriously brings back to life
the faithless gleam of Being,
— its horror and all it denies.")

"M'introduire dans ton histoire…" (page 190)

Published in *La Vogue* of 13-20th June 1886. It's worth noting that this poem, rather than "Mes bouquins refermés sur le nom de Paphos…", was placed at the very end of the 1887 *Poésies*.

L. 3-4 — *S'il a du talon nu touché / Quelque gazon de territoire*: the "talon nu" might recall the use of "foot" or "feet" as a biblical euphemism for "penis";[186] "gazon" is slang for "pubic hair".

L. 9-10 — *Dis si je ne suis pas joyeux / Tonnerre et rubis aux moyeux*: T.S. Eliot echoes line 10 in section II of 'Burnt Norton':

> Garlic and sapphires in the mud
> Clot the bedded axle-tree

— these lines first appeared in an early draft (dedicated to Mallarmé) of Eliot's short poem 'Lines for an Old Man'.[187] Eliot's lines also recall the "boue et rubis"

---

[186] See James Orr, *International Standard Bible Encyclopaedia*, vol. II, p. 1126.
[187] See Ronald Bush, 'Modern/Postmodern: Eliot, Perse, Mallarmé and the Future of the Barbarians', in *Modernism Reconsidered*, eds. Robert Kiely and John Hildebidle,

of 'Le Tombeau de Charles Baudelaire'.

L. 13 — *Comme mourir pourpre la roue*: presumably a reference to the setting sun, which only *seems* to die every night, in a purple sunset.[188]

"À la nue accablante tu…" (page 192)

Published in the *Obole littéraire* (a magazine sold to raise money for winter shelters for the homeless) of 15th May 1894. The Barbier and Millan *Poésies* includes a facsimile of the poem, in Mallarmé's handwriting, and with an illustration by Fernand Khnopff, taken from the Berlin journal *Pan* of April-May 1895.

L. 2 — *Basse de basalte et de laves*: "basse" is either an adjective meaning "low" and qualifying "la nue", or a feminine noun meaning "a reef".

L. 7 — *les épaves*: "flotsam", "wreckage", "unclaimed property"; "une épave" can also be a human wreck. *Les Épaves* was the title of a pamphlet by Charles Baudelaire, including the six poems censored from the first edition of *Les Fleurs du mal*.

L. 9 — *cela*: either the pronoun "that", or the past historic of the verb "celer" ("to conceal").[189] In the latter interpretation, "abolit" and "cela" both take "Quel sépulcral naufrage" for subject, and line 9 might be translated "Or concealed the fact that, mad for the want…" Hans-Jost Frey's essay 'Spume'[190] is a particularly clear guide to the sonnet's complexities.

L. 10 — *perdition*: both the nautical term for a ship in distress, and a more general sense of physical or spiritual ruin or loss.

191-214, 211 n.52. The Eliot poem, as published, ends "Tell me if I am not glad!"

[188] See A.R. Chisholm, 'Mallarmé: M'introduire dans ton histoire', *French Studies*, vol. 30 (1976), 170-172, 171.

[189] E. Noulet, *Vingt poèmes de Stéphane Mallarmé*, 245. Noulet's interpretation is based on that of Luigi de Nardis.

[190] *Yale French Studies*, 74 (1988), 249-260.

L. 12 — *Dans le si blanc cheveu qui traîne*: Karlheinz Stierle[191] suggests that the shipwreck is specifically that of youth, and the poem inspired by a lover's first white hair.

"Mes bouquins refermés sur le nom de Paphos…" (page 194)

Published in *La Revue indépendante* in January 1887.

L. 1 — *bouquins*: "small, old or unimportant books". Littré lists two very Mallarméan homonyms for "bouquin": "an old goat or satyr" and "the mouthpiece of a tobacco pipe".

L. 1 — *Paphos*: In Ovid's *Metamorphoses*, Book X, the sculptor Pygmalion falls in love with one of his own ivory statues. Venus changed the statue into a living woman, who bore Pygmalion a daughter, Paphos (after whom the city was named).[192]

L. 3 — *Une ruine, par mille écumes bénie*: The city of Paphos was the legendary site of the birth of Aphrodite from sea-spray,[193] and had a temple consecrated to Her. Pliny the Elder (*Naturalis Historia*, 36.4) gives two stories of adolescents falling in love with statues of Aphrodite (though not at Paphos) and staining them with *écume*.

---

[191] Karlheinz Stierle (tr. Sibylle Kisro), 'Position and Negation in Mallarmé's "Prose pour des Esseintes"', *Yale French Studies*, 54 (1977), 96-117, 114.

[192] In some texts of Ovid, Paphos is said to be Pygmalion's son rather than his daughter. The statue-wife is traditionally named Galatea ("she who is milk-white"), though this tradition only dates to the mid eighteenth century. Book X of the *Metamorphoses* also includes the story of Paphos's son Cinyras (for whom see the notes to 'Scène: Hérodiade'), and that of Hyacinthus (see line 4 of the present sonnet). In lines 82-84 of the 'Scène', Hérodiade imagines herself seen as if sculpted.

[193] Hesiod, *Theogony*, line 196 derives her name from a Greek word meaning "foam-born"; Aphrodite's birth was as motherless as that of Pygmalion's wife. By the end of the *Poésies*, the verse-foam of 'Salut' still hasn't lost its virginity, but finds itself at the centre of a profoundly ambiguous network of representations of physical, divine and artistic generation.

L. 6 — *nénie*: in ancient Rome, a form of funeral lamentation by professional mourners (Littré).

L. 7-8 — compare the white frolic, and the false landscape, with Marcel Duchamp's 1946 work *Paysage Fautif* ("Faulty Landscape"), an amoeboid blot of human sperm mounted on black satin.[194]

L. 12 — *guivre*: a heraldic term for a serpent or dragon. See the notes to 'Scene: Hérodiade' for another wyvern.

L. 13 — *éperdûment*: also "madly", as in "éperdûment amoureux" ("madly in love").

L. 14 — *antique amazone*: according to some texts of Strabo's *Geography* (Book XI), the city of Paphos was founded by Amazons.[195]

---

[194] See Gavin Parkinson, *The Duchamp Book*, 63ff.

[195] See E. Noulet, *L'Œuvre poétique de Stéphane Mallarmé*, 445. Strabo, *Geography*, 11.5.4 opens with a list of cities reputed to have been founded by Amazons. According to the Loeb Classical Library edition (Volume 5: Books 10-12, 236 n.1), some manuscripts of the work add Paphos to the end of the list (the standard text has the word "τάφοι" ("tombs") here instead).

SELECT BIBLIOGRAPHY

Primary sources:

Correspondance complète 1862-1871 suivi de Lettres sur la poésie 1872-1898, ed. Bertrand Marchal (Paris: Gallimard, 1995). A very useful one-volume selection of Mallarmé's letters. Cited in the notes as *Correspondance*.

Igitur, Divagations, Un coup de dés, ed. Bertrand Marchal (Paris: Gallimard, 2003).

Mallarmé-Whistler: Correspondance, ed. C.P. Barbier (Paris: A.G. Nizet, 1964).

Les Noces d'Hérodiade. Mystère, ed. Gardner Davies (Paris: Gallimard 1959).

Œuvres Complètes, ed. Henri Mondor and G. Jean-Aubry (Paris: Gallimard, 1945). An obsolete edition and by no means complete, but the only one which can currently be found second-hand at a reasonable price... Cited in the notes as *OC* (all references are to the 1951 edition).

Œuvres Complètes volume 1, *Poésies*, ed. C.P. Barbier and Charles Gordon Millan (Paris: Flammarion, 1983). Planned as a multi-volume edition, of which only the first volume appeared. A chronological arrangement of all known versions of Mallarmé's *Poésies* and *Vers de circonstance*, with detailed textual (but no interpretive) notes.

Œuvres Complètes tomes 1 and 2, ed. Bertrand Marchal (Paris: Gallimard, 1998 and 2003). Most of the relevant notes from this edition can also be found in the Marchal (ed.) *Poésies*.

Poésies, ed. Lloyd James Austin (Paris: Flammarion, 1989). Includes a very fine introductory essay by Austin (in French).

Poésies, ed. Bertrand Marchal (Paris: Gallimard, 1992). The best current separate edition.

(Littré) in the notes indicates a reference to the great 19th century *Dictionnaire de la langue française*, compiled by Émile Littré. The online version at http://francois.gannaz.free.fr/Littre/accueil.php is an indispensible resource.

Books on Mallarmé (including collections of essays):

Jill Anderson (ed.), *Australian Divagations: Mallarmé & the 20th Century* (New York: Peter Lang, 2002).

L.J. Austin, *Poetic principles and practice* (Cambridge University Press, 1987)
———, *Essais sur Mallarmé* (ed. Malcolm Bowie; Manchester University Press, 1995)

Leo Bersani, *The Death of Stéphane Mallarmé* (Cambridge University Press, 1982).

Malcolm Bowie, Alison Fairlie and Alison Finch (eds.), *Baudelaire, Mallarmé, Valéry: new essays in honour of Lloyd Austin* (Cambridge University Press, 1982).

Malcolm Bowie, *Mallarmé and the Art of Being Difficult* (Cambridge University Press, 1978).

A.R. Chisholm, *Mallarmé's Grand Œuvre* (Manchester University Press, 1962).

Robert Greer Cohn, *Toward the Poems of Mallarmé* (expanded edition, Berkeley and Los Angeles: University of California Press, 1980).
——— (ed.), *Mallarmé in the Twentieth Century* (Associated University Presses, 1998).

Gardner Davies, *Les "Tombeaux" de Mallarmé: essai d'exégèse raisonnée* (Paris: Librairie José Corti, 1950).
———, *Mallarmé et le drame solaire: essai d'exégèse raisonnée* (Paris: Librairie José Corti, 1959).

Pascal Durand, *Poésies de Stéphane Mallarmé* (Paris: Gallimard 1998).

Wallace Fowlie, *Mallarmé* (University of Chicago Press, 1953).

Austin Gill, *The Early Mallarmé*, volumes 1 and 2 (Oxford: Clarendon Press, 1979 and 1986).

David Kinloch and Gordon Millan (eds.), *Situating Mallarmé* (Bern: Peter Lang, 2000).

Heath Lees, *Mallarmé and Wagner: Music and Poetic Language* (Aldershot and Burlington: Ashgate Publishing, 2007).

Nikolaj d'Origny Lübecker, *Le sacrifice de la sirène: «Un coup de dés» et la poétique de Stéphane Mallarmé* (København: Museum Tusculanum Press, 2003).

(No author listed), *Mallarmé et les "Siens"* (Sens: Musées de Sens, 1998).

Charles Mauron, *Mallarmé l'Obscur* (Paris: Librairie José Corti, 1968).

———, *Introduction to the Psychoanalysis of Mallarmé* (tr. Archibald Henderson, Jr. and Will L. McLendon; Berkeley and Los Angeles: University of California Press, 1963).

Gordon Millan, *A Throw of the Dice: The Life of Stéphane Mallarmé* (London: Secker and Warburg, 1994).

Jean-Claude Milner, *Mallarmé au tombeau* (Vendôme: Éditions Verdier, 1999).

Henri Mondor, *Vie de Mallarmé* (Paris: Gallimard, 1941).

E. Noulet, *L'Œuvre poétique de Stéphane Mallarmé* (Paris: Librairie E. Droz, 1940).

———, *Vingt poèmes de Stéphane Mallarmé* (Geneva: Librairie Droz, 1967).

Marshall C. Olds, *Desire Seeking Expression: Mallarmé's "Prose pour des Esseintes"* (Lexington, KY: French Forum, 1983; free pdf edition at the University of Nebraska, Lincoln website http://digitalcommons.unl.edu/modlangfrench/).

Roger Pearson, *Unfolding Mallarmé: The Development of a Poetic Art* (Oxford: Clarendon Press, 1996).

———, *Mallarmé and Circumstance: The Translation of Silence* (Oxford University Press, 2004).

———, *Stéphane Mallarmé* (London: Reaktion Books 2010).

Yves Peyré (ed.), *Mallarmé 1842-1898: Un destin d'écriture* (Paris: Gallimard/Réunion des Musées Nationaux, 1998).

Graham Robb, *Unlocking Mallarmé* (New Haven and London: Yale University Press, 1996).

F.C. St. Aubyn, *Stéphane Mallarmé* (updated edition, Boston: Twayne Publishers, 1989).

Michael Temple, *The Name of the Poet: Onomastics and Anonymity in the*

Works of Stéphane Mallarmé (Exeter: University of Exeter Press, 1995).

André Vial, *Mallarmé: Tétralogie pour un enfant mort* (Paris: Librairie José Corti, 1976).

Other books cited:

Albert Barrère, *Argot and Slang; a new French and English dictionary of the cant words, quaint expressions, slang terms and flash phrases used in the high and low life of old and new Paris* (London: Whittaker & co, 1889; online version at www.archive.org).

E.M. Beaumont, J.M. Cocking and J. Cuickshank, *Order and Adventure in Post-Romantic French Poetry: Essays Presented to C.A. Hackett* (Oxford: Basil Blackwell, 1973).

Charles Bernstein, *My Way: Speeches and Poems* (University of Chicago Press, 1999).

Nicolas Boileau-Despréaux, *Œuvres complètes* (Paris: Gallimard, 1966).

A.R. Chisholm: *Towards Hérodiade: A Literary Genealogy* (Melbourne University Press, 1934).

Jacques Derrida, *Acts of Literature* (ed. Derek Attridge; New York: Routledge, 1992).

————, *Dissemination* (translated by Barbara Johnson; University of Chicago Press, 1981).

Edward J.H. Greene, *T.S. Eliot et La France* (Paris: Éditions contemporaines, 1951).

Jacob Grimm, *Teutonic Mythology* (translated in four volumes by James Steven Stallybrass; London: W. Swan Sonnenschein & Allen, 1880-1888; online version at www.archive.org).

Denis Hollier and Jeffrey Mehlman (eds.), *Literary debate: texts and contexts* (New York: The New Press, 1999).

Barbara Johnson, *The Critical Difference: Essays in the Contemporary Rhetoric of Reading*, Baltimore and London: The Johns Hopkins University Press, 1980).

————, *A World of Difference*, Baltimore and London: The Johns Hopkins University Press, 1987).

Robert Kiely and John Hildebidle (eds.), *Modernism Reconsidered* (Cambridge, Massachusetts: Harvard University Press, 1983).

Lorédan Larchey, *Les Excentricités du langage* (4th edition, Paris: E. Dentu, 1862; online version at www.archive.org).

Cecily Mackworth, *English Interludes : Mallarmé, Verlaine, Paul Valéry, Valery Larbaud in England, 1860-1912* (London: Routledge and Keegan Paul, 1974).

Debra N. Mancoff, *Flora Symbolica: Flowers in Pre-Raphaelite Art* (New York: Prestel Publishing, 2003).

James Orr, *The International Standard Bible Encyclopaedia* (Chicago: The Howard-Severance Company, 1915; online version at www.archive.org).

Jean Pommier, *Dialogues avec le passé: études et portraits littéraires* (Paris: Librairie A.-G. Nizet, 1967).

Gavin Parkinson, *The Duchamp Book* (London: Tate Publishing, 2008).

Christopher Prendergast (ed.), *Nineteenth-Century French Poetry : Introductions to Close Reading* (Cambridge University Press, 1990).

Michael Riffaterre, *Semiotics of Poetry* (London: Methuen 1980).

Denis Saurat, *Perspectives* (Paris: Éditions Stock, Delamain et Boutelleau, 1938).

Karl Shuker, *Dragons: a Natural History* (New York: Simon & Schuster, 1995).

Benn Sowerby, *The Disinherited: The Life of Gérard de Nerval 1808-1855* (London: Peter Owen, 1973).

Jack Spicer, *My vocabulary did this to me: the collected poetry of Jack Spicer* (eds. Peter Gizzi and Kevin Killian; Middletown, CT: Wesleyan University Press, 2008).

Marie-Thérèse Stanislas, *Geneviève Mallarmé-Bonniot* (Saint-Genouph: Librairie A.-G. Nizet, 2006).

Arthur Symons, *The Symbolist Movement in Literature* (New York, E.P Dutton & Co, inc., 1958).

Paul Verlaine, *The Cursed Poets* ('Les Poètes maudits', translated by Chase Madar; Los Angeles: Green Integer, 2003).

Websites

http://www.geocities.jp/mal_archives/MalDB.html — a Mallarmé bibliography.

http://gallica.bnf.fr/ — the Bibliothèque nationale de France.

http://persee.fr/ — free access to many French-language academic journals.

http://www.archive.org/details/texts — the Internet Archive text collection.

Other translations of the *Poésies*, including anthologies with substantial Mallarmé content:

Daisy Aldan, *To Purify the Words of the Tribe: The Major Verse Poems of Stéphane Mallarmé with Un coup de Dés jamais n'abolira le Hasard* (Huntington Woods, Michigan: Sky Blue Press, 1999).

E.H. and A.M. Blackmore, *Stéphane Mallarmé: Collected Poems and Other Verse* (Oxford University Press, 2006).

Keith Bosley, Mallarmé: *The Poems* (Harmondsworth: Penguin, 1977).

Hayden Carruth, *L'Après-midi d'un faune* (Tucson: Ironwood Press, 1981; also in Carruth's *Collected Shorter Poems*).

Ciaran Carson, *The Alexandrine Plan* (Winston-Salem: Wake Forest University Press, 1998). Includes translations of nine Mallarmé poems.

Mary Ann Caws (ed.), *Stéphane Mallarmé: Selected Poetry and Prose* (New York: New Directions, 1982). Includes twenty-four poems translated by several hands.

Charles Chadwick, *The Meaning of Mallarmé* (Aberdeen: Scottish Cultural Press, 1996). Not strictly a translation, but a book of expanded interpretive paraphrases of most of the *Poésies*.

Brian Coffey, *Salut: versions of some sonnets of Mallarmé* (Dublin: Hard Pressed Poetry, 1988). A selection of five poems.

————, *Poems of Mallarmé* (Dublin/London: New Writers' Press/The Menard Press, 1990). A further selection of fifteen poems.

Arthur Ellis, *Stéphane Mallarmé in English Verse* (London: Jonathan Cape, 1927).

Angel Flores (ed.), *An Anthology of French Poetry from Nerval to Valéry* (New York: Doubleday, 1958; republished 2000). Includes twenty-seven poems translated by several hands.

Roger Fry, *Stéphane Mallarmé: Poems* (London: Chatto and Windus, 1936).

Anthony Hartley, *Mallarmé* (Harmondsworth: Penguin, 1965). Prose translations.

Jim Hanson, *Stéphane Mallarmé's Poems* (online at www.jimhanson.org).

James Kirkup, translations of seventeen poems (online at www.brindin.com).

A.S. Kline, *Mallarmé: Selected Poems* (online at www.brindin.com).

David Lenson, *Hérodiade* (in *The Massachusetts Review*, vol. 30, no. 4, Winter 1989, 573-588. A translation of the 'Ouverture ancienne', 'Scène' and 'Cantique de saint Jean').

C.F. MacIntyre, *Stéphane Mallarmé: Selected Poems* (Berkeley and Los Angeles: University of California Press, 1957).

Dorothy Martin, *Sextette: Translations from the French Symbolists* (London: The Scholartis Press, 1928). Includes five poems.

Clark Mills, *Herodias* (Prairie City, Illinois: J.A. Decker, 1940; reprinted New York: AMS Press, no date. A translation of the Hérodiade 'Scène').

Robert L. Mitchell, *Corbière, Mallarmé, Valéry: Preservations and Commentary* (Saratoga, CA: Anma Libri 1981). Includes ten poems.

Andrei Molotiu, *The Afternoon of a Faun* (Calgary, Alberta: No Press 2010).

Christine North, *Mallarmé* (Enfield: Perdika Press, 2006). A selection of eleven poems.

David Paul, *Poison and Vision: Poems and Prose of Baudelaire, Mallarmé and Rimbaud* (University of Salzburg Press, 1996). Includes twenty-four poems.

Enid Rhodes Peschell, *Four French Symbolist Poets* (Athens: Ohio University Press 1981). Includes twenty-five poems.

William Rees (ed. and trans.), *French Poetry 1820-1950* (Harmondsworth: Penguin, 1990). Includes ten poems in prose translation.

David Scott, *Mallarmé Sonnets* (Exeter: Shearsman Books, 2008).

Arthur Symons, *Stéphane Mallarmé: Poésies* (ed. Bruce Morris; Edinburgh: The Tragara Press, 1986). A selection of ten poems.

Henry Weinfield, *Stéphane Mallarmé: Collected Poems* (Berkeley and Los Angeles: University of California Press, 1994).

Grange Woolley, *Stéphane Mallarmé 1842-1898* (Madison, NJ: Drew University, 1942). Includes eighteen poems as an appendix to a critical study.

In addition, the critical studies by Robert Greer Cohn and Wallace Fowlie include literal translations of many of the *Poésies*. Walter Conrad Arensberg's poetry collection *Idols* (Boston and New York: Houghton Mifflin & Co, 1916) includes a remarkable early translation of 'L'Après-midi d'un faune'; another appears in Aldous Huxley's *The Defeat of Youth and Other Poems* (Oxford: B.H. Blackwell, 1918) and a third in James H. Rubin's *Manet's Silence and the Poetics of Bouquets* (London: Reaktion Books, 1994; translation by Rubin with Robert Harvey and Harry Gilonis).

The translations by E.H. and A.M. Blackmore, Keith Bosley, Anthony Hartley and Henry Weinfield also include Mallarmé's prose poems and 'Un coup de Dés jamais n'abolira le Hasard'. A complete translation, by Barbara Johnson, of Mallarmé's prose book *Divagations* was published by Harvard University Press in 2007: this can be supplemented by the selections in *Mallarmé in Prose* (ed. Mary Ann Caws; New York: New Directions, 2001) and in *Mallarmé: Selected Prose Poems, Essays and Letters* (tr. Bradford Cook; Baltimore: The Johns Hopkins Press, 1956). Robert Greer Cohn's *Mallarmé's Divagations: A Guide and Commentary* (New York: Peter Lang, 1990) is also useful. A *Selected Letters of Stéphane Mallarmé*, edited and translated by Rosemary Lloyd, was published by the University of Chicago Press in 1988.

A note on the text

I've chosen not to relegate to an appendix those poems which have been added to the *Poésies* since the first "complete" edition of 1899: the ordering and selection of the poems here is essentially that of the 1945 Pléiade *Œuvres complètes*. What the book loses thereby in methodological soundness is offset, I hope, by the convenience of being able to read the 'Hérodiade' poems, the 'Chansons bas' and the 'Tombeaux' together in sequence. The reader should consult the 1992 Gallimard *Poésies* (for the 1899 text), and the 2006 Oxford University Press *Collected Poems and Other Verse* (which follows Mallarmé's 1894 maquette for the *Poésies*, the last arrangement known to have been approved by the poet himself).

The following poems in this book were not included the 1899 *Poésies*: "Une négresse par le démon secouée…", 'Ouverture ancienne d'Hérodiade', 'Cantique de saint Jean', 'Éventail de Méry Laurent', "Dame / sans trop d'ardeur à la fois enflammant…", "Ô si chère de loin et proche et blanche, si…", "Rien, au réveil, que vous n'ayez…", "Si tu veux nous nous aimerons…", 'Le Cantonnier', 'Le Marchand d'ail et d'oignons', 'La Femme de l'ouvrier', 'Le Vitrier', 'Le Crieur d'imprimés', 'La Marchande d'habits', 'Petit air (Guerrier)', "Sur les bois oubliés quand passe l'hiver sombre…" and "Toute l'âme résumée…"

The Verlaine 'Tombeau' ("Le noir roc courroucé que la bise le roule…") and the Vasco da Gama sonnet ("Au seul souci de voyager…") were written after the maquette for what would become the 1899 *Poésies* had been delivered to the publisher. They seem to have been added to the book by Mallarmé's daughter Geneviève, some time after the poet's death in September 1898.

Acknowledgements

Earlier versions of many of these translations were first published in, or on, the following journals and websites: *Axolotl*, *Black Box Manifold*, *Chicago Review*, *Free Verse*, *Gare du nord*, *onedit*, *Poems and Poetics*, *Plantarchy*, *Quid*, *Shearsman*, *Translation Ireland* and *Reconfigurations*. Versions of fifteen poems appeared as a pamphlet, *Before and After Mallarmé* (Glasgow: Survivors' Press, 2005). My thanks to the editors and publishers, Joshua Adams, Tim Atkins, Bobby Baird, Tony Frazer, Michael Hansen, Scott Howard, Justin Katko, John Kearns, Joshua Kotin, Gerry Loose, Alice Notley, the late Douglas Oliver, Adam Piette, Luke Roberts, Jerome Rothenberg, Keston Sutherland and Jon Thompson. Grateful thanks are due to the Scottish Arts Council for a writer's bursary which supported me through the latter stages of the work. The cover image, an unfinished drypoint portrait of Mallarmé by James McNeill Whistler (c. 1891-2) is reproduced by kind permission of the Hunterian Art Gallery, University of Glasgow. Thanks also to the Keeper of Special Collections, Glasgow University Library, for permission to quote an editorial from the issue of *The Whirlwind* in the Whistler archive. The library's two extraordinary Mallarmé collections (Whistler's and that of the late Professor Carl Barbier) are a sustaining source of wonder, and should be far better known. Thanks to Keith Tuma for agreeing to publish these translations as a book, to Dana Leonard for the care and clarity she brought to its making, and to Madge Duffey for designing the cover. Thanks to Jacqueline Kari for help with the proofing. All translations from French texts in the *Scholia* and afterword are my own, unless otherwise noted. For their help, encouragement and suggestions, and for difficult questions both asked and answered, I would like to thank Maggie Graham, David Kinloch, Tom Leonard, Gerry Loose, Ian Patterson, Geoff Squires, Mark Weiss and, above all, Robin Purves. This book is for Robin, Zahida, Maya and Stéphane.

Afterword

> "The literal translation bears only the same relation to the American as
> the skeleton of a young girl would to the sweet and rosy girl herself.
> The skeleton proves only that she was neither hunchbacked nor bandy-
> legged: the lines in French, likewise, reveal that the piece is lacking in
> no basic quality. In seeing the one, we do not know how sweet and
> rosy was the flesh that covered it, in reading the other, we have no
> suspicion of the beauty of the lugubrious rhythm. The "jamais plus"
> is an immense effect in the American: he says "never more" which is
> pronounced "néveur môre" [;] it is one of the most beautiful English
> words because of its very sad idea, and it is a lugubrious sound which
> imitates admirably the guttural cawing of the sinister visitor. So much
> for the words; everyone judges from the heart."
>
> > (Mallarmé's note to his first translation of
> > Poe's 'The Raven', from the notebook enti-
> > tled 'Glanes' ["Gleanings"], 1860.)[196]

These are unashamedly semantic translations of a poet whose best writing seems
designed to put a semantic translator to shame. They exist because I wanted to
find my own way in to the *Poésies*, a book I could at first make hardly anything
of but whose strangeness and sparkle and density and smallness would not
allow me to leave alone. I first tried to translate a Mallarmé poem in 1992 (it
was "Toute l'âme résumée..."), and a few others followed later in the 1990s.
Every poem seemed eventually to open a door onto another, and by 2004 I
knew I wanted to translate them all. The translation was, above all, my way
of proving to myself that I actually had read the poems, and of slowing that
reading down as far as I possibly could. The project held on to me through
several years when not much else in the way of writing seemed possible, and I
owe it more than I or anyone else will ever know. Translating Mallarmé is a job
that can't possibly be finished (it's up to the reader to decide whether or not I

---

[196] Quoted in Austin Gill, *The Early Mallarmé*, vol. 2, p.9.

ever really began), but for now, for this book, this is it.

All polemical generalisations about translation are so easily refuted that it's hard to know where to start. These translations were done in the conviction that a translation of Mallarmé should at least be allowed to sound like interesting modern poetry, and that the strict (or even the very lax) use of rhyme and regular metre is one of the surest ways of forbidding that from happening. I know that rhyme is an absolutely fundamental property of Mallarmé's poetry, but that very centrality seems to me to argue against the rhymed translation of it. Rhyme is one of the most powerful resources available to a poet engaged in original composition: it stands second only to syntax as a means of moving forward into the potential space which will be the poem. The poet who has written the first line of a Petrarchan sonnet already knows something about the phonetic properties of line eight; the first two lines of Mallarmé's sonnet "Ses purs ongles très haut dédiant leur onyx..." predicted the rhyme sounds of the last two. I don't think that rhyme is capable of playing anything like the same generative and exploratory role in the making of a translation. The semantic ghost of a completed poem in the source language already haunts the space of the translation — the translator knows what it is that has to be said, and in these circumstances rhyme can have only the negative function of distorting it in the service of virtuosic display. To paraphrase Robert Frost, it's tennis, and should concern no-one.[197]

Arthur Symons's vibrantly weird translation of 'Prose (pour des Esseintes)'[198] might be as close as we'll ever get to a truly creative rhymed translation of Mallarmé. Here are two representative stanzas:

> The site of a hundred Irises,
> That knew not what grimacing Mummer

---

[197] Yves Bonnefoy's essay 'On the Translation of Form in Poetry', *World Literature Today*, vol. 53 no 3 (Summer 1979), 374-379, makes a better job of a similar case.

[198] Stéphane Mallarmé, *Poésies*, translated by Arthur Symons, 39-43. A complete edition of Symons's (mostly unpublished) Mallarmé translations is long overdue.

> Uttered the name of our Paradises
> To the sound of the trumpets of the summer

[and]

> Glory of long desire, Ideas
> Excited in me the sense of beauty
> In seeing the Irises like Medeas
> Surge out of the depths of duty.

The Mummer, the Paradises, the sense of beauty and the Medeas (*more than one* Medea: the poverty of the rhyme somehow makes it even better) are all summoned into existence by an utterly fearless determination to rhyme at all costs. Symons ends by deriving an English poem on the immortality of the Spirit from a French original which seems to me to be about the almost-immortality of paper. Most other rhymed translations sound timid by comparison, the rhymes often approximate and the rhyme-schemes usually radically simplified — sufficiently foregrounded to be distracting and misleading, while never finding the courage to amaze.

Traditional French verse looks so much like traditional English verse on the page that it would seem logical, in translating, simply to substitute one of our old established metres for one of theirs — English iambic pentameter for French alexandrine, say. I think this approach seriously understates the "otherness" of the French line: nothing in post-mediaeval English corresponds to the role played in French prosody by the "e muet", the orthographic "e" which remains silent in everyday speech but is counted as a full syllable when it occurs before a consonant in a line of verse. There's something magical about the way in which a sequence of words like

> Contre le marbre vainement de Baudelaire

(from Mallarmé's 'Le Tombeau de Charles Baudelaire') swells from eight to twelve syllables as soon as it's perceived as a line of verse. This feeling for verse as something which has been breathed into, inflated or made effervescent by the sighing of the mute e, is one of the things that lies behind the famous opening line of the *Poésies*,

> Rien, cette écume, vierge vers

— and, remembering that the distinguishing characteristic of a poet (in Plato's *Ion*) is that s/he has been breathed into by the gods, the line of French verse comes to seem remarkably poet-like, more human than material. In 'Don du poème', Mallarmé emerges from an insomniac night with a helpless, new-born poem which he invites his wife to breast-feed.

I went through a phase of saying that the line I was aiming for in the translations (of the longer-lined poems at least) formed a kind of interference-pattern between English pentameter and French alexandrine, but really I've been playing it by ear. I've tried to make the English lines as short as they can be and as long as they need to be, in the belief that this is the best way to keep pace with the highly variable semantic yield of the French. Much of the interest, for me, has been in watching what happens to my sense of what a line in English can be, when almost all of my attention has been taken up with the meaning (or meanings) of the corresponding French. My fantasy would have made, of these translations, poems whose form really would be never more than an extension of their content — though I'm aware of how often the limitations of my own ear have dragged them back towards an approximately iambic baseline.

I've tried, wherever possible, to keep a line-by line correspondence between the English and French. A good case can be made for prose translations (of the kind Mallarmé himself made of the poems of Edgar Allan Poe, or Anthony Hartley made of Mallarmé), but it seems silly to throw away the linebreak, when linebreaks can so often be translated. Every change that I've made in the sequencing of a group of lines represents a failure of nerve (I feel most guilty about the second tercets of "Quelle soie aux baumes de temps..." and

"M'introduire dans ton histoire..."), but without failures of nerve we would all already have died.

The verbal music of these translations, if they have any, is not that of the originals: "Le vierge, le vivace et le bel aujourd'hui..." in my translation is no longer a "sonnet in i". My hope is that by giving the English language its head, and trusting it to bear a weight of syntactic complexity which is almost (but not quite) Mallarméan, I've created a space where the poems are able to take on something of an independent life in English. I didn't consciously set out to put a quadruple internal rhyme on "eyes" in the last four lines of 'Funeral Toast', or to frame the second poem of Mallarmé's 'Triptych' in the English-only wordplay of "Arisen ... / ... a rose", but I'm glad those things happened: if they hadn't, there would be little point in showing the poems to you.

At a time when a younger contemporary like René Ghil was building an arid and prescriptive system of correspondences between instruments of the orchestra, vowel and consonant effects in poetry, and specific emotions, Mallarmé stressed that his understanding of the music of poetry was quite different:

> ... it is not from elementary sonorities through brass, strings, wood, undeniably but from the intellectual word at its apogee that there must result, with plenitude and obviousness, as the totality of relations existing in everything, Music.[199]

And again:

> Employ Music in the Greek sense, signifying, basically, Idea or rhythm between relations; more divine there than in its public or symphonic expression.[200]

A music of the Idea, a relational music, seems at least potentially a translatable

---

[199] 'Crise de vers', in *Igitur, Divagations, Un coup de dés*, 258.
[200] Letter to Edmund Gosse, 10th January 1893. *Correspondance*, 614.

music, to be approached by cleaving as closely as possible to the sense and syntax of the French — translating literally when that can be made to work, and inventively when it can't. Much is lost in any translation, much more in translating from a poet as rich in undecidabilities as Mallarmé. The Scholia are my attempt to reinstate some of the lost complexity. I'm a glossator, not a scholar, but I've tried to point to as much useful secondary literature as I can, to add observations of my own and to limit myself to what I hope is a permissible minimum of pareidolia. Staring at the same hundred-page book for twenty years can lead to unusual mind-states; it seems best to say so.

The most contentious aspect of the book might, in the end, be its presentation as a parallel text. Mallarmé seems to have interpreted the parallelism of book-pages as something very like a series of equals-signs, implying the profound internal unity of his ideal content (and/or the arbitrary equivalence of all its component parts).[201] His translations of Edgar Allan Poe were always published in French only — the sole exception being the 1875 separate edition of 'Le Corbeau / The Raven',[202] where four strands of content (Poe's English, blank pages, Manet's illustrations and Mallarmé's French) were alternated page by page, in such a way that English and French were never lined up on facing pages as implied equivalents. Given Mallarmé's penchant for seeing the book as a tomb (or a coffin) for the writer's soul, I'm afraid that a parallel text might sentence him to eternal unrest in a grim parody of the "twin sepulchre" in his poem "Sur les bois oubliés quand passe l'hiver sombre..." The poem contains its own answer: a "pierre" (for Peter) is a burden light enough to be lifted by the finger of a bored, dead person. Murmur Mallarmé's name, not mine, until nightfall, and you too shall have the visit. Often.

Glasgow, September 2011.

---

[201] See his essay 'Le Livre, instrument spirituel', in *Divagations*.

[202] Page scans of the 1875 edition can be viewed on the Library of Congress website, http://lccn.loc.gov/48033816

ABOUT THE AUTHOR

STÉPHANE MALLARMÉ was born in Paris on 18th March 1842, the son of Numa Mallarmé (1805-1863) and Élisabeth Desmolins (1819-1847). He had one sister, Maria (1844-1857). After a short spell in the Registry Office at Sens, he trained as a teacher of English, working at schools in Tournon, Besançon and Avignon before settling in Paris in 1871. He married Maria Gerhard (1835-1910) in 1863, and they had two children, Geneviève (1864-1919) and Anatole (1871-1879). He retired from teaching in 1893, and died, at Valvins (now Vulaines-sur-Seine), on 9th September 1898. His books include *Poésies* (limited "photolithographic" edition 1887, trade edition 1899), the prose book *Divagations* (1897), school textbooks on the English language (*Les Mots anglais*, 1878) and on mythology (*Les Dieux antiques*, 1879), and a French translation of the poems of Edgar Allan Poe (1888). He wrote widely on contemporary literature, visual art and theatre, and briefly became the editor of (and main contributor to) a fashion magazine, *La Dernière mode* (1874). His groundbreaking visual poem, 'Un coup de Dés jamais n'abolira le Hasard' ("A throw of the Dice never will abolish Chance"), was published in the journal *Cosmopolis* in 1897, and in book form in 1914. Works published posthumously include the prose tale *Igitur* (1925) and the surviving notes towards three unfinished projects: *Le Livre* ("The Book", 1957), *Les Noces d'Hérodiade* ("The Marrying of Hérodiade", 1959) and *Pour un Tombeau d'Anatole* ("For Anatole's Tomb", 1961).

PETER MANSON lives in Glasgow, Scotland. His books include *Between Cup and Lip* (also from Miami University Press), *For the Good of Liars* and *Adjunct: an Undigest* (both from Barque Press). Another book, *Poems of Frank Rupture*, is due in 2012. More information at www.petermanson.com

Other titles in the Miami University Press Poetry Series

Ralph Angel | *Neither World*

Judith Baumel | *Now*

Molly Bendall | *Ariadne's Island* | *Dark Summer*

Debra Bruce | *What Wind Will Do*

Mairéad Byrne | *Talk Poetry*

John Drury | *Burning the Aspern Papers* | *The Disappearing Town*

Aaron Fogel | *The Printer's Error*

Fergal Gaynor | *VIII Stepping Poems & other pieces*

Frederick Goodwin | *Virgil's Cow*

Kate Knapp Johnson | *This Perfect Life* | *Wind Somewhere, and Shade*

Larry Kramer | *Brilliant Windows*

Peter Manson | *Between Cup and Lip*

Steve Orlen | *The Bridge of Sighs* | *Kisses*

Hugh Seidman | *People Live, They Have Lives* | *Selected Poems: 1965–1995*

Aleda Shirley | *Long Distance*

Jim Simmerman | *Kingdom Come* | *Moon Go Away, I Don't Love You No More*

Jeffrey Skinner | *Gender Studies*

Keith Tuma, Ed. | *Rainbow Darkness: an anthology of African American poetry*

Nance Van Winckel | *After A Spell* | *Beside Ourselves* | *The Dirt*

View our complete catalog at www.muohio.edu/mupress